CHALLENGES for CHILDREN

Creative Activities for Gifted and Talented Primary Students

Carole Cook   Jody Carlisle

*Illustrated By
Dave Dillon*

The Center for Applied Research in Education, Inc.
West Nyack, New York 10995

© 1985 by
The Center for Applied
Research in Education, Inc.
West Nyack, New York

All rights reserved.

Permission is given for individual teachers to reproduce the student activity pages and illustrations for classroom use. Reproduction of these materials for an entire school system is strictly forbidden.

Library of Congress Cataloging in Publication Data

Cook, Carole
　Challenges for children

　Includes index.
　1. Gifted children— Education.　2. Activity programs in education.　3. Creative thinking (Education)
I. Carlisle, Jody.　II. Title.
LC3993.C59 1985　　　371.95′3　　　84-21432

ISBN 0-87628-196-X

Printed in the United States of America

FOR OUR PARENTS

Otto and Ruby Sponsler
Reginald and Madelyn Stafford

ABOUT THIS BOOK

The purpose of *Challenges for Children: Creative Activities for Gifted and Talented Primary Students* is to teach the primary-age gifted and talented child specific skills that will later enable him or her to become an independent problem solver. These skills are taught through the use of a wide range of activities in the basic content areas of language arts, math, social studies, and science, as well as specialized sections of the book including independent challengers, library/study skills, and creative arts. Although categorized by content area, the activities are interdisciplinary and often require integration of several skills.

Designed for use by the primary teacher, the activities in the book may also be appropriate for use by specialists in the field of gifted education. They were developed for kindergarten through third grade children with above-average abilities or children with special interests in a particular curriculum area. Many of the activities are appropriate for children in all primary grades as they are designed to elicit responses, develop critical thinking skills, and provide hands-on experiences for children.

Each of the seven sections in the book is followed by a wide range of activities from bulletin board suggestions and reproducible pages to publishing a newspaper and completing an independent study. The activities have been arranged from the easiest to the most difficult in each section, but can be used in any order desired, and provide for a wide range of oral and written responses. For easy use, each unit includes an illustrated overview of the section, with ready-to-use teaching activities and reproducible activity pages that are ready for immediate classroom use. A career activity for each content area has been included to allow the children an opportunity to demonstrate their understanding of the skills taught within the unit.

One of the most beneficial uses of the book is that it enables you to select an activity based on the classroom curriculum, a specific skill, or a specific content area to meet the needs of children in your classroom who have special abilities and talents. Within each content area there are activities that will provide valuable learning experiences for individuals as well as small groups and that provide you with an opportunity to utilize a variety of teaching techniques inlcuding classroom projects, learning centers, and independent study.

HOW TO USE THIS BOOK

OVERVIEW AND SKILLS

Much has been written on how to teach critical thinking in the regular classroom, and it is our philosophy that critical thinking can only be taught if the child possesses specific skills. It is also our philosophy, however, that the teaching of isolated skills is only a means to an end. It is not until a child can successfully apply and integrate the skills to solve a problem that he or she has truly learned to be a critical thinker. Therefore, it is necessary to begin at the beginning with the primary child and teach the skills in isolation before the child is ready to learn to integrate these skills and apply them to a specific problem-solving situation. Some of the specific skills that help prepare the child to become a critical thinker and have been targeted in the activities in this book are:

finding out/locating	observing/recording
gathering/collecting	experimenting/predicting
describing/translating	comparing/analyzing
planning/organizing	relating/judging
arranging/selecting	evaluating/deciding
categorizing/classifying	imagining/redesigning
hypothesizing/interpreting	composing/creating
constructing/designing	

The activities compiled in this book are designed as a springboard. If you take each activity and present it based only on what is written, and do not personalize it for your own use based on both the child's and your needs, then the goal of this book has not been attained. We want you to build from the responses of the children, even if takes the lesson in a different direction from that which is outlined in this book. We want these activities to be stimulators for many real learning experiences in your classroom.

It may also become necessary for a specialist to intervene and work with the bright and gifted children in order for the children to utilize the skills they have learned in isolation to solve problems. This is mainly because of the restraints placed upon you with regard to classroom grouping, size, limited time, and predetermined curricular expectations outlined by the school system.

After being exposed to these isolated skills and having applied them in the classroom, the child should be given more intensive opportunities to integrate the skills and apply them to problems of the real world.

CHARACTERISTICS OF THE GIFTED AND TALENTED

Many definitions could be quoted to answer the question, "Who are the gifted and talented?" For instance, the United States Office of Education has its own definition; many states, counties, and even school systems have their own definitions. It would, therefore, be difficult for us to give one definition, for like all "special" populations of children, definitions differ according to many variables. For the purpose of this book, the "Classroom Behaviors Checklist" on pages 7-9 helps identify children who will benefit from the activities included in this book.

It is recommended that this Checklist be used only as a screening device. It is in no way designed to be used for formal identification of gifted and talented students. We would encourage you to observe children in the classroom and, after becoming familiar with each child, read the characteristics on the "Classroom Behaviors Checklist" and write the name or names of individual children who come to mind beside each characteristic. After the names have been recorded beside each characteristic, go back over the Checklist and write down the names that continually reappear. These children are potential candidates for the activities included in this book. This does not, however, eliminate any other child who has a particular interest or desire to participate in any of these activities.

Teacher's Name _____   Date _____

CLASSROOM BEHAVIORS CHECKLIST

Directions: Read each characteristic below. Write the name or names of students who come to mind.

Social/Emotional

A. Organizes groups easily.

   1. _____   2. _____   3. _____

B. Demonstrates leadership qualities.

   1. _____   2. _____   3. _____

C. Understands subtle humor.

   1. _____   2. _____   3. _____

D. Chooses to do activities alone.

   1. _____   2. _____   3. _____

E. Has excellent control of feelings or shows extreme rage at others' shortcomings.

   1. _____   2. _____   3. _____

F. Persists in tackling a difficult job.

   1. _____   2. _____   3. _____

G. Chooses the company of older children.

   1. _____   2. _____   3. _____

H. Is a perfectionist.

   1. _____   2. _____   3. _____

I. Is a daydreamer.

   1. _____   2. _____   3. _____

J. Is able to find alternate solutions in difficult situations.

   1. _____   2. _____   3. _____

K. Expects truth, honesty, and fairness.

   1. _____   2. _____   3. _____

L. Works in disorganized organization.

   1. _____   2. _____   3. _____

© 1985 by The Center for Applied Research in Education, Inc.

Physical/Intellectual

A. Is physically well coordinated.

 1. _____ 2. _____ 3. _____

B. Attempts tasks too difficult for the age.

 1. _____ 2. _____ 3. _____

C. Has an extended attention span.

 1. _____ 2. _____ 3. _____

D. Reads well above grade level.

 1. _____ 2. _____ 3. _____

E. Asks a lot of questions.

 1. _____ 2. _____ 3. _____

F. Uses large vocabulary.

 1. _____ 2. _____ 3. _____

G. Shows knowledge of an abundance of general information and trivia.

 1. _____ 2. _____ 3. _____

H. Juggles tasks easily.

 1. _____ 2. _____ 3. _____

I. Is interested in collections.

 1. _____ 2. _____ 3. _____

J. Sees parts of a whole.

 1. _____ 2. _____ 3. _____

K. Demonstrates abstract reasoning ability.

 1. _____ 2. _____ 3. _____

L. Enjoys experimenting in many areas.

 1. _____ 2. _____ 3. _____

M. Plays a musical instrument.

    1. _____   2. _____   3. _____

N. Demonstrates excellent drawing ability.

    1. _____   2. _____   3. _____

O. Enjoys creative writing or word games.

    1. _____   2. _____   3. _____

P. Has good long-term memory.

    1. _____   2. _____   3. _____

Q. Dislikes repetition and set routine.

    1. _____   2. _____   3. _____

R. Persists in pursuing special interests.

    1. _____   2. _____   3. _____

S. Grasps new concepts easily.

    1. _____   2. _____   3. _____

T. Is original and creative in art, music, and drama.

    1. _____   2. _____   3. _____

Potential Gifted/Talented Students

List the names of students whose names reoccur many times.

1. _____
2. _____
3. _____
4. _____
5. _____
6. _____
7. _____
8. _____
9. _____
10. _____

IDENTIFYING INTERESTS

In order to determine the interests of individual students, an interest inventory should be administered to *all* children in any classroom. This will enable you to capitalize on the interests of the children when developing the curriculum and creating activities for daily use.

A sample "Interest Inventory" (see page 11) is included here, but should be personalized according to the ages of the children and community location. Your talents should also be explored and capitalized upon.

INTEREST INVENTORY

My name is _____.

My favorite food is _____.

My favorite quiet game is _____.

When I'm loud and active, I like to play _____.

My favorite TV show is _____.

I like to read about: 1. _____, 2. _____,

and 3. _____.

The music I like best is _____.

This year I wish we could learn more about: 1. _____,

2. _____, and 3. _____.

I do not enjoy studying about: 1. _____, 2. _____,

and 3. _____.

In art I enjoy _____.

In music I really like _____.

On projects I like working with others ☐ or alone ☐ .

© 1985 by The Center for Applied Research in Education, Inc.

CLASSROOM MANAGEMENT TIPS

Classroom teachers often ask "How can I find the time to instruct students with special needs?"

There are several ways of helping the gifted and talented child during the course of the teaching day. Some of these are:

- Have a parent volunteer come in to help with a specific project.
- Group a few together for instruction on a specific topic.
- Use older gifted and talented children to supervise some projects.
- Involve the librarian in specific library projects.
- Seek the aid of the art or music teacher for creative arts.
- Give three or four days of instruction in specific content areas and use one day for creative expansion.

Some ideas on classroom arrangement that could prove helpful would be to:

- Put materials in a specific place and identify each with labels and signs for the students to use easily.
- Have a separate work space for your special students.
- Have self-checking lists available to lighten your load.
- Allow students to help decide specific areas of learning.
- Make sure there are activities for all ability levels in centers.
- Make daily/weekly contracts.
- Organize and initiate independent reading projects.

We hope the activities and suggestions offered in this book will help develop both your students' and your own creativity!

Carol Cook
Jody Carlisle

CONTENTS

About This Book   2

How to Use This Book   3
    Classroom Behaviors Checklist–5
    Interest Inventory–9

Section I: LIGHT UP YOUR CLASS WITH LANGUAGE ARTS • 17

Activity	Skill	Page
Mouthy Monsters	imagining	18
My Teddy Bear	composing	22
A Picture and a Thousand Words	describing/creating	23
Crazy Rhymes	redesigning	24
Mixed-Up ABCs	arranging/organizing	27
Newspaper	categorizing/creating/composing	29
News Flash	interpreting/developing	31
Rag A. Muffin	redesigning	32
Clothesline Analogies	interpreting/evaluating	34
Picture Analogies	interpreting/evaluating	36
Word Analogies	interpreting/evaluating	37
More Word Analogies	interpreting/evaluating	38
Shoes for Sale	designing	39
Write, Write, Write	collecting	41
So You Want to Be a Writer	composing/evaluating/selecting	42
Author at Work	composing	43

Section II: BRILLIANT MATH IDEAS • 45

What Comes Next?	arranging/interpreting	46
What's Next?	arranging/interpreting	47
Fruity Line-Up!	arranging/interpreting	48

Activity	Skill	Page
Next in Line!	arranging/interpreting	49
Number Line-Up	arranging/interpreting	50
The Number Train I	arranging/interpreting	51
The Number Train II	arranging/interpreting	52
The Line-Up!	arranging/interpreting	53
Big, Big Brontosaurus	hypothesizing/translating	54
Coats of Many Colors	analyzing/evaluating	55
Shoe Power	interpreting/evaluating	56
Sweet Treats	money problem solving	57
Making Change	money problem solving	59
Use Your Head, Then Use Your Calculator	money problem solving	59
Timely Math	interpreting	60
Minute by Minute	interpreting	61
What's for Dinner?	planning	62
Shopping at the School Store	money problem solving	63
Christmas Wish List	money problem solving	64
Clock Puzzlers	interpreting	65
Time Out	analyzing/evaluating	66
Egg-citing Survey	collecting/analyzing	67
Banking Is My Business	planning/recording/evaluating	70
Having Your Own Checking Account	planning/recording/evaluating	71
Balancing My Own Checkbook	recording	73
Borrowing Money	money problem solving	74

Section III: TURN ON WITH SOCIAL STUDIES • 75

Activity	Skill	Page
What's Inside?	hypothesizing	76
All About Me	finding out	77
I Want to Know About Me!	finding out/composing	78
My Family Tree	finding out	79
I Want to Know About You!	finding out/composing	80
Where Am I?	interpreting/designing	81
Communication	interpreting	82
How Communication Has Changed	finding out	83
Sign Language	relating/interpreting	84
Body Language	relating/interpreting	85
Braille	relating/interpreting	87
Future Communication	relating/interpreting	88
Extra, Extra! Read All About It	creating	91

Activity	Skill	Page
Bonjour! Buenos Dias!	creating	93
Tid Bits About _____	finding out	95
Oldies But Goodies	classifying/describing	97
Can You Dig It?	hypothesizing/interpreting/evaluating	98

Section IV: REALLY SHINE WITH SCIENCE • 103

Activity	Skill	Page
Animalology	creating/redesigning	104
Insects	finding out/creating	107
Hear Ye! Hear Ye!	experimenting/predicting	108
The Wheel	experimenting/constructing/creating	109
Kitchen Wheels	observing/recording/evaluating	110
Machines with One Wheel	observing/recording/evaluating	111
Three-Wheel Wonders	observing/recording/evaluating	112
Up, Up, and Away	organizing/constructing/interpreting	114
A Plant Is What It Eats!	experimenting/predicting	115
Red Celery?	observing/recording	116
Spiders, Spiders Everywhere!	collecting	118
Rain, Rain Go Away	recording/analyzing/evaluating	120
Sunny, Cloudy and Rainy Days	analyzing/predicting	123
Our Friendly Sun	predicting	126
Hooting About Polluting	judging/analyzing	129
For the Birds	observing/recording/evaluating	130
The Microscope Mystery	observing/analyzing	133
Microscope Magic	observing/predicting/recording	135
Ants, Ants Everywhere	observing/recording/analyzing	137
Our Ant Farm	observing/predicting/recording	139
I Want to Be a Vet	finding out/interpreting/evaluating	141
Jane and Kiki	analyzing/interpreting	142

Section V: GLOW WITH LIBRARY/STUDY SKILLS • 145

Activity	Skill	Page
Be a Bookworm	locating	146
Knowing Your ABCs	decoding	147
Animal Train	arranging	148
Phone Book Madness	locating	149
Look for It	locating	150
Cue Cards	decoding/applying/locating	151
S-A-T Catalog	creating	152

Activity	Skill	Page
Use Your Encyclopedia	collecting/hypothesizing	154
Loch Ness Monster	collecting/hypothesizing	156
Abominable Snowman	collecting/hypothesizing	157
Big Foot	collecting/hypothesizing	158
The Shape of Things	gathering/creating	159
It Happened Just So!	finding out/creating	160
Wild, Wild Animals	creating	161
Little Red Riding Hood	analyzing	164
Library Detective	certificate of award	169
Announcing	planning/analyzing/creating	170

Section VI: SPOTLIGHT ON CREATIVE ARTS • 171

Activity	Skill	Page
Shapes Galore	Creating	172
Heads-Up	designing/constructing	173
Junk Art	deciding/creating	174
Poetic Snow People	creating	175
Pantomime Kids	interpreting/creating	177
Slide Show	creating	179
Comic Carnival	designing/creating	180
Let's Make Music	composing	181
Chime Practice	interpreting/creating	182
My Chime Time	composing	183
Music Masters	finding out/comparing	184
Learning About the Masters	finding out/evaluating	185
Experimenting with Writing	experimenting	188
Haiku	creating	189
Quiet on the Set!	creating	191
Making Pottery	finding out/hypothesizing/creating	193
All About Pottery	finding out/hypothesizing	194

Section VII: BRIGHTEN YOUR DAY WITH INDEPENDENT CHALLENGERS • 197

Activity	Skill	Page
A Treasure Hunt	locating/deciding/creating	198
A Flying Teapot?	creating	200
To Pollute or Not to Pollute?	analyzing/planning	202
My Country 'Tis of Thee	categorizing/designing	205
Experimenting	experimenting/predicting	207
Bird Watchers	observing/recording/evaluating	209
Library Search	deciding	212
Water, Water Everywhere	observing/predicting/deciding	214

Activity	Skill	Page
Tall Plans	deciding/creating/evaluating	218
Choosing a Career	deciding/selecting	220
My Interview of a _____	finding out	223
Careers of the Future	selecting/predicting	225
My Career of the Future	predicting	226

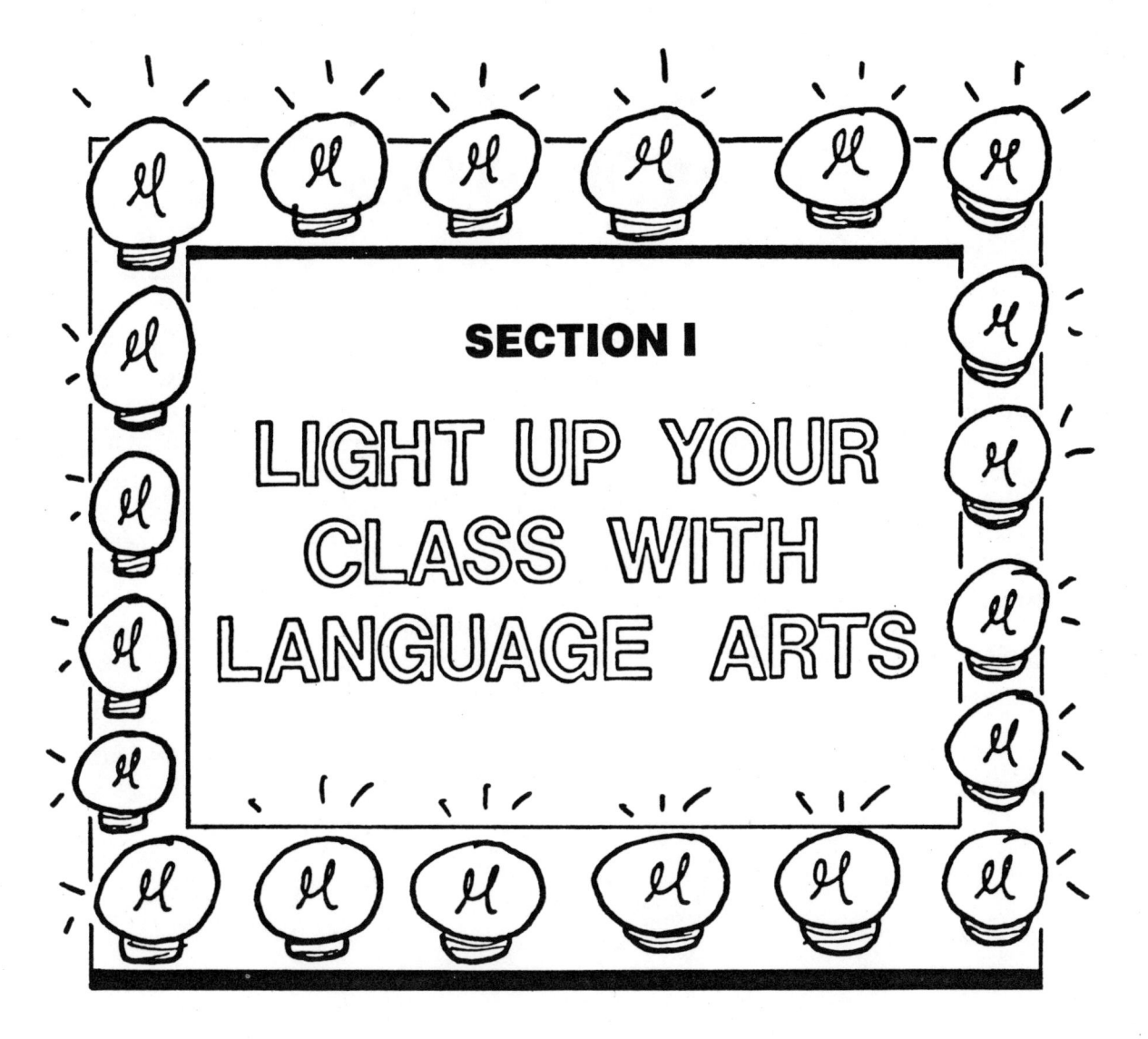

SECTION I
LIGHT UP YOUR CLASS WITH LANGUAGE ARTS

Many bright and gifted children come to school already reading, and most have taught themselves to read through their own symbol system. They usually have many shortcuts for decoding words and often have a difficult time explaining exactly how they decode them. These children are interested in all forms of vocabulary development and enjoy humorous language patterns. They accept as a challenge the idea of analogies, creating poetry, and developing their own stories. Therefore, we have chosen to include activities encouraging both oral and written communication, utilizing old forms of communicating in a new way, and drawing relationships between words and sentences.

Within the language arts section, the children are given many opportunities to create through writing. They can develop a slogan or commercial, create a tongue twister or analogy, maintain a collection of their writings, and even try their hand at getting their own writings published.

It is important to remember that children be given many opportunities to express themselves, for the more opportunities children have, the better their products will become.

MOUTHY MONSTERS

Bright children usually have no trouble learning their beginning sounds. Therefore, you can develop the sounds with the use of monster tongue twisters and some thought-provoking questions.

Enlarge the following monsters and make charts to be used with a small group of students. After introducing the letter and its sound, read the tongue twister to the group. You will be surprised how quickly they will learn the tongue twister as well as develop an extensive sight vocabulary. After they know the tongue twister, ask the questions listed below each drawing to encourage creative thinking.

After using the four mouthy monsters, have the group develop their own tongue twister about a beginning sound. You may want to start a twister and have them fill in the blanks at first. For example: "Terrible Tom told a tall tale of…"

After they create their own tongue twisters, have the students create their own monsters to depict their characters.

MICKEY MONSTER MADE A MILKSHAKE IN THE MIDDLE OF MILLIE MONSTER'S MAROON MITTEN!

- What game do you think Mickey Monster would like to play? Why?
- Explain how you would make a milkshake. List all the steps.
- What else could Mickey Monster make that begins with an "M"?
- Draw a picture of Millie Monster and her maroon mitten.

HANDY HARRY HAD
A HANDFUL OF HORNS
HANDED TO HIM
BY HIS HORSE

- Name all of the kinds of horns that you can think of.
- What kinds of horns did Handy Harry have?
- How many horns is a handful? Can every monster hold the same number of horns?

SILLY SARA SANG
A SONG SWEETLY AS
SHE SAT SO STILL
FOR HER SUPPER

- Why do you think Silly Sara is so fat?
- What song might Silly Sara sing?
- Do you think you would like Silly Sara's singing? Why?

BILLY BLOB BOUGHT A BIG BUNCH OF BAKED BAGELS FOR BONNIE'S BREAKFAST.

- What is a blob? A bagel?
- How many might be in a bunch? Why?
- Make a picture in words of what Monster Bonnie looks like.

MY TEDDY BEAR

Try a creative approach to a discussion. Select four or five children to come to the front of the room. Explain to each of them that they are to pretend to be a stuffed animal of some kind. It can be one they have at home or one they have always wished they could have. Be sure to encourage them to think a few minutes before responding to the questions you are going to ask. Ask each child the following question: "If you could be any kind of stuffed animal, what would you be?"

After allowing time for each child to respond, ask each of the following questions, giving the children enough time to think and respond.

- "Tell me about yourself. What color are you? What are you made of?"
- "Who is your owner? What is your owner like? How are you treated?"
- "Somehow a part of your body (arm, leg, ear, etc.) came off. Explain how it happened and how you feel."
- "You know stuffed animals can't talk, but suppose they could. What would you tell your owner?"

After the children have had several opportunities to be different objects and answer similar questions, their answers will become more creative. You may want them to draw a picture of the stuffed animal that they were during the activity.

A PICTURE AND A THOUSAND WORDS

Children love to make booklets about almost anything. To begin this project, write a few topics on small pieces of paper and put them into a hat. Some topics you might choose are:

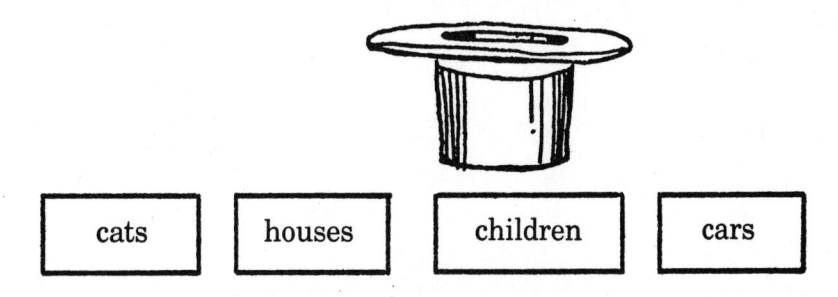

| cats | houses | children | cars |

Each child chooses a slip of paper (several children may have the same topic) and begins to look for magazine pictures about that topic. Each child will need to find five or six pictures, and paste one picture on each page of the booklet.

Each student now finds words in the magazine or newspaper that would describe the picture, and pastes them under it. Then, using these words, the student writes a sentence at the bottom of the page to describe the picture.

CRAZY RHYMES

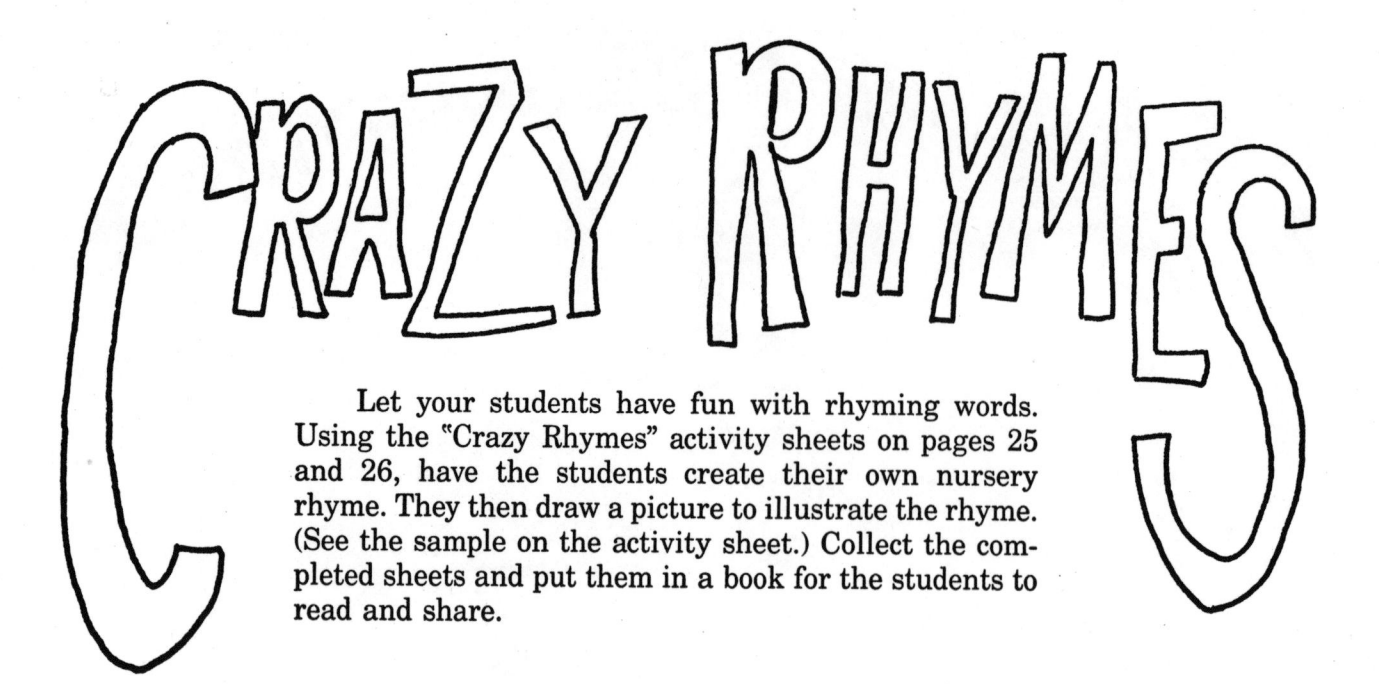

Let your students have fun with rhyming words. Using the "Crazy Rhymes" activity sheets on pages 25 and 26, have the students create their own nursery rhyme. They then draw a picture to illustrate the rhyme. (See the sample on the activity sheet.) Collect the completed sheets and put them in a book for the students to read and share.

CRAZY RHYMES

There was an old woman
Who lived in a __hut__
She had so many __puppies__
She thought she'd go __nuts__

1. There was an old woman
   Who lived in a zoo.
   She had so many _____
   She didn't _____.

2. There was an old _____
   Who lived in a pan.
   He ate so many _____
   He _____ _____.

3. There was an old woman
   Who lived in a shoe.
   She had so many _____
   She _____.

4. There was an old king
   Who lived in a _____
   He had _____
   He _____.

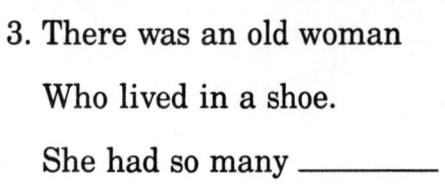

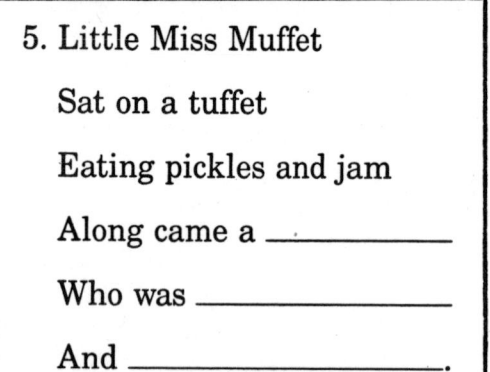

5. Little Miss Muffet
   Sat on a tuffet
   Eating pickles and jam
   Along came a _____
   Who was _____
   And _____.

6. Little Miss Grouch
   Sat on a couch
   Eating her curds and whey
   Along came a grinch
   Who _____
   And _____.

7. Little Miss Muffet
   Sat on a tuffet
   Eating her bowl full of soup
   Along came a _____
   And sat down _____
   And _____.

8. Little Miss King
   Sat on a _____
   Eating her curds and whey.
   Along came a _____
   And sat very humbly _____
   And _____.

Now create your own rhyme from any of your favorite nursery rhymes by changing the rhyming words!

26

MIXED-UP ABCs

A box of alphabet cereal or macaroni can be used for many different activities. For bright preschool youngsters, it is an easy way to begin working with letter and sound identification. From the identification stages, the children can then begin forming words. Once they are forming words, they can learn a few connectors and use these words in sentences. Every child in your group can participate at the same time, learn by actually manipulating the letters, and even (in the case of cereal) "eat their own words" when the activity is completed. Styrofoam meat trays come in handy for this activity. This way, you can also limit the number of letters each child has to work with. The brighter or more advanced the child, the larger the number of letters he or she can be given to use in the activity.

Once students can form sentences with the letters, they are ready to create their own textured story. To improve small muscle control, children may use cereal or ABC macaroni to write the entire story, write words at random in their story, or write words that they would like to emphasize in the story. Here is one example:

I found a LARGE frog in my yard. He had BULGING eyes and SMOOTH skin. When I tried to put him in a GLASS jar he took a LONG leap and was gone.

Their story paper can then be glued onto a shaped sheet of construction paper for display.

NEWSPAPER

Newspapers can be used in many different ways after they have been read for the news they contain. Here are some activities you can try.

Activity 1

Give each child a sheet of newspaper that has varying size print and words. (Avoid using want ads.) Now ask the children to find as many words as they know and underline them. It is a good idea to have a time limit and to spot check to make sure the students know the words they underlined. This is a good activity to do when you have an aide to assist you.

Activity 2

Have the children share their words. Write each word on a card. After the words are shared, categorize the words in different ways, such as by color, shape, content, etc. After working with the words, the children will begin to develop a substantial sight vocabulary. Now group the words into three categories:

1. names of persons, places, things (nouns)
2. action words (verbs)
3. describing words (adjectives)

You will be surprised how easy it is to teach bright kindergarteners and first graders the parts of speech. You are now ready to show them how to put the words together to make sentences. Have the children move the cards around. If they want to add a new word that they can't spell, give them a blank card and let them draw a picture. Let the other children figure out the sentence. Then add the word to their vocabulary.

Activity 3

Using the sight words and some pictures, develop a rebus story to share with the children. Allow time for the children to figure out the story individually and then go over the story with the group. Discuss proper story form and the idea that a good story always has a beginning, middle, and end. With the group, create a rebus story using their word cards, pictures, and large chart paper. When they have mastered how to construct a story properly, move on to Activity 4.

Activity 4

After a considerable vocabulary has been built, have the children again cut out words that they recognize from the newspaper. Using large sheets of manila paper, have the children create rebus stories using the words they have cut out, and drawings of the missing words. Tell the children you will be looking for sentence structure, nouns, verbs, and adjectives.

When the children have completed their stories, ask them to trade with another student to read the stories. Then share the stories in a group.

Activity 5

After several rebus stories have been written, begin a new lesson by giving each child or pair of children an unusual object that must be included in the story. Some examples may be a marshmallow, pencil, paper clip, cookie, tissue, or small box. You will be surprised at how quickly a marshmallow can become a character—"The marshmallow boy was soft and round." It might be a good idea to model the way you can develop a story around a particular object, such as a rubber band. The rubber band can instantly become an inchworm that always wanted to be able to stretch more than an inch.

Then just sit back, give the children time to create, and you will have delightful stories. After using one unusual object, you may want to have the students include two or three different objects. Don't forget about the possibility of having some of your outstanding stories published in children's magazines. Check the front of the magazines for specific details.

Activity 6

For children who really become interested in the newspaper and would like to find out more about it, use the "News Flash" activity sheet on page 31. If interest is high enough, this would be an excellent time to create your own classroom newspaper.

News Flash

1. What are today's headlines?
   _____
   _____
   _____
   _____

2. Why do we have headlines?
   _____
   _____
   _____
   _____

3. Why are the headlines so big?
   _____
   _____
   _____
   _____

4. If a space ship landed in your town, what do you think the headlines of your newspaper would say?
   _____
   _____
   _____
   _____

RAG A. MUFFIN

Read the story of "Cinderella" to the children. Then ask them to retell the story using their own words to insure that they know the sequence of events.

Ask the children to use their own magic wands to change Cinderella from a housemaid to "Rag A. Muffin," the chimney sweep. Brainstorm with the children about potential changes in the story. Some of the following questions would need to be clarified about Rag A. Muffin:

1. Rag A. Muffin was a chimney sweep who always looked like _____.
_____.
2. Rag A. Muffin wanted to go to _____.
3. The _____ helped Rag A. Muffin.
4. Rag A. Muffin wore _____ to _____.
5. Rag A. Muffin rode in a _____ made from a _____.
6. A _____ found Rag A. Muffin's _____.
7. At the end of the story, Rag A. Muffin was a _____.

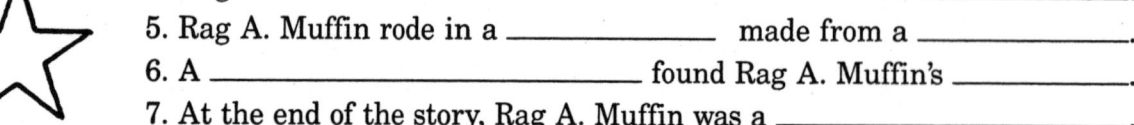

After discussing many varied possibilities about "Rag A. Muffin," have the children create a story about the character, using the basic plot of the fairy tale "Cinderella." You may want to use the activity sheet on page 33 to help the children visualize "Rag A. Muffin."

DRAW A PICTURE
OF
RAG A. MUFFIN

CLOTHESLINE ANALOGIES

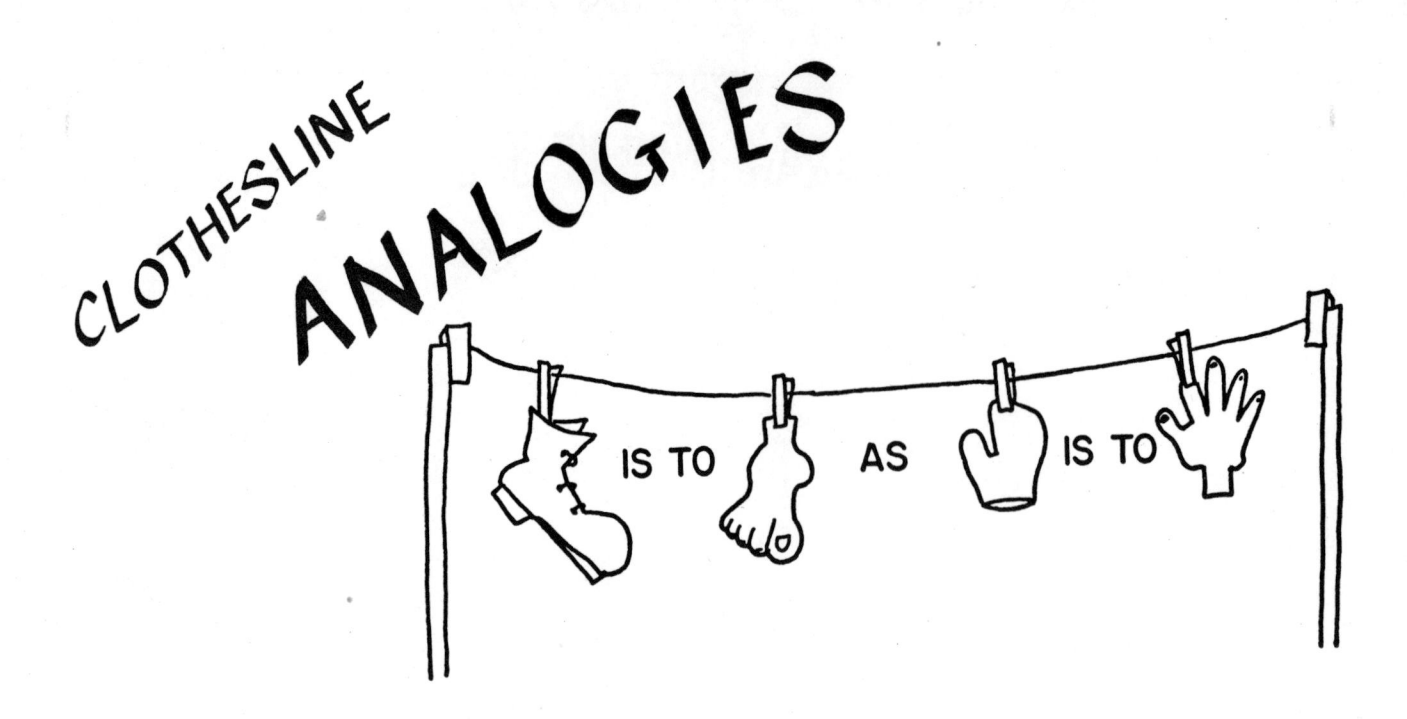

Words can go together in many different ways. Children easily learn about antonyms (hot and cold), synonyms (large and big), and homonyms (see and sea). Bright students can also easily identify relationships between words. Why not teach your students to see analogies between words and to even create simple ones of their own?

When first introducing analogies, you will need to discuss various kinds of relationships between words. You can ask the children what relationship a shoe has to a foot and a mitten to a hand. You can talk about how a pencil relates to a piece of paper, or chalk to a blackboard. The key is to use relationships that a child would easily relate to, as well as recognize.

Now you are ready for clothesline analogies. Somewhere in your classroom, hang a short clothesline. On the clothesline, hang the word "is to" and "as" in the proper places.

Have picture/word cards that the children can pin up on the clothesline to make analogies. Begin by limiting the number of choices they have to make. You may want to start with only two sets of analogies.

34

[dog] IS TO BARK AS [cat] IS TO MEOW

[fire] IS TO HOT AS [ice] IS TO COLD

Have the children practice making the relationships. As the relationships become more familiar and the students more confident, add additional word pairs. You may also want the students to try creating their own analogies.

After much practice, you may want to utilize the three activity sheets on pages 36-38 to reinforce the students' understanding of analogies.

PICTURE ANALOGIES

Directions: Cut out the pictures at the bottom of the page. Glue them in the correct box.

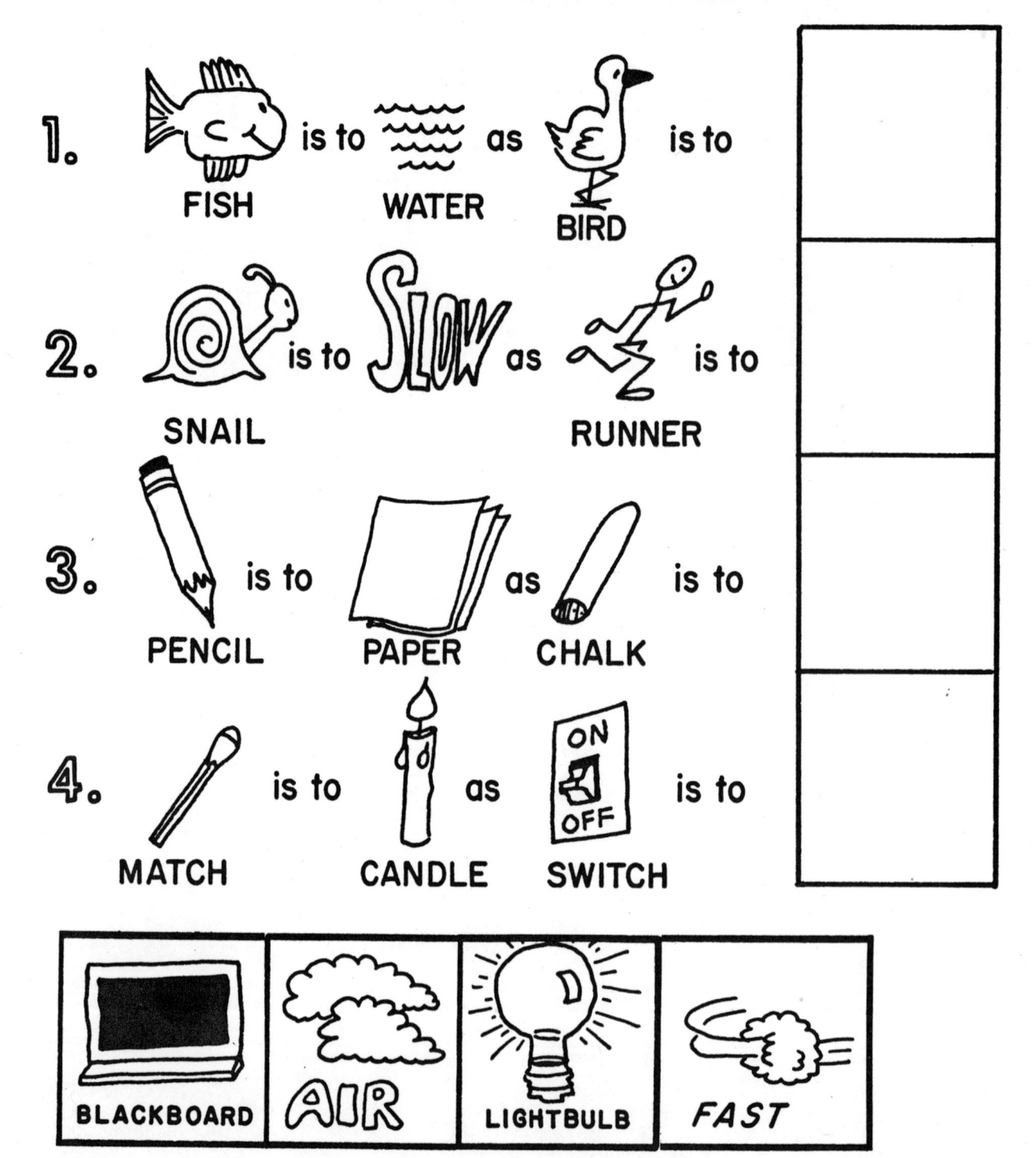

1. FISH is to WATER as BIRD is to _____

2. SNAIL is to Slow as RUNNER is to _____

3. PENCIL is to PAPER as CHALK is to _____

4. MATCH is to CANDLE as SWITCH is to _____

| BLACKBOARD | AIR | LIGHTBULB | FAST |

36

© 1985 by The Center for Applied Research in Education, Inc.

Word Analogies

DIRECTIONS: Choose the correct word. Write it in the blank.

Sugar   Bed   Bark   Foot   Hot

1. COAT is to COLD as BATHING SUIT is to _____.

2. DOG is to _____ as CAT is to MEOW.

3. SITTING is to CHAIR as LYING is to _____.

4. FINGER is to HAND as TOE is to _____.

5. SWEET is to _____ as SOUR is to LEMON.

More Word Analogies

Directions: Choose the correct word. Write it in the blank.

CAR   TRAIN   SMELL   FOOT   MITTEN

1. HORSE is to BUGGY as ENGINE is to _____.

2. FLOWER is to _____ as MUSIC is to HEAR.

3. _____ is to HAND as SHOE is to _____.

4. FOOD is to BODY as GASOLINE is to _____.

☆ Make up one analogy of your own.

5.

Shoes for Sale

Children are constantly bombarded with TV commercials and slogans. You probably have children in your classroom who can act out a commercial or share a popular product slogan with the class. Discuss with your class what makes a good commercial/slogan, such as rhyming words, catchy phrases, and putting words to a tune. Talk about the impact of commercials/slogans on their parents and themselves, especially around Christmas time. Allow time for some of the children to act out their favorite commercials or share a slogan.

Then divide the class into small groups to create a slogan/commercial to sell their favorite pair of shoes. Have each group make a presentation to the class when they are ready. Have the class select their favorite commercials/slogans. Perhaps they can vote. You might even discuss TV ratings and why some commercials/slogans continue to be used while others are cut. As a special activity, have the winning commercial script or slogan sent to the appropriate shoe company for evaluation. Who knows??? Maybe it will be a real hit!

WRITE! WRITE! WRITE!

As a teacher, you are always after children to write. Those writings are shared and sent home; collected, graded, and sent home; crumpled up in the back of the desk or tossed in the trash can.

In order for you and the child to see the progression of his or her writing (punctuation, sentence/paragraph formation, fluency, creative thought, etc.), you need to keep samples of the work.

At the beginning of the year, the children should create a writing portfolio. A large sheet of posterboard will make an excellent portfolio. Have the children fold the posterboard in half and tape the sides with colored plastic tape.

Allow time for each student to decorate his or her portfolio. Throughout the year, samples of the student's work should be kept. This will enable you to show how the student's writings have progressed. The portfolio is an excellent tool for diagnosis of problems as well as strengths, and will give you the opportunity to work with each student on his or her own individual level. It is also an excellent tool for evaluation and sharing during parent conferences.

SO YOU WANT TO BE A WRITER

Many people have always wanted to write, but wait too long before beginning to develop their writing skills. Like any other talent, writing skills must be developed early and practiced in order to gain proficiency. You have probably had the opportunity to work with a number of students who seem to possess writing talent. These are the students who should be encouraged to complete the "Author at Work" activity sheets on pages 43 and 44. This activity should be attempted only if the child has an interest in having the work published, and if the writing appears to have potential.

As mentioned earlier, the child should already be maintaining a writing portfolio. The child will identify his or her most precious works, or those most admired by others. You will need to collect several current issues of children's magazines, such as *Cricket* and *Jack and Jill*. Check these issues to make sure they contain children's writings. After finding a number of magazines, check the front for instructions for submitting student works. Specific instructions are generally outlined. Make a list of potential publishers and their manuscript requirements.

Name _____   Date _____

AUTHOR AT WORK

1. Look at the magazines your teacher has collected for you. Read several of the stories in each of the magazines. Decide which magazine you like best and tell your teacher.
2. Look through your writing portfolio with your teacher. Select your best story or stories.
3. Write a letter to the publisher of the magazine and tell about your story. (Include when you wrote it, why you wrote it, and why you think it would be a good story to publish in the magazine.) Share the letter with your teacher.
4. Copy your letter again and correct any spelling and punctuation mistakes. Be sure to write it like a proper business letter. (See the sample.) Share it with your teacher.

```
                                    ABC ELEMENTARY SCHOOL
                                    1234 LEARNING ROAD
                                    ANYTOWN, USA 12345

        MR. JOHN DOE
        PUBLISHER
        BIG CITY BOOKS
        LARGE TOWN, USA 12345

        DEAR MR. DOE
                                    SINCERELY
                                    JOE SMITH
```

5. Address an envelope for mailing your letter and writings. Be sure to put a stamp on the envelope. (See the sample.)

```
JOE SMITH
1234  LEARNING ROAD
ANYTOWN, USA 12345

              MR. JOHN DOE
              PUBLISHER
              BIG CITY BOOKS
              LARGE TOWN, USA  12345
```

6. Gather your letter and writings and place them in the envelope. (Be sure to follow the instructions from the publisher. You may need to send two copies or a stamped, self-addressed envelope to return your writings if they are not used.)
7. Place your envelope in the mail.
8. Now the hardest part of all—waiting and waiting and waiting. Don't be discouraged if at first you don't succeed. Try another publisher or another story. (You might send your stories to two or three publishers, and that way, the waiting won't seem so long.)

SECTION II

BRILLIANT MATH

$X = MC^2$

6%

$$\begin{array}{r} 2 \\ +1 \\ \hline \end{array}$$

$$\begin{array}{r} 4 \\ \times 2 \\ \hline \end{array}$$

1 X 2

IDEAS

Developing an understanding and appreciation for the language of mathematics is the most important goal for bright students to accomplish in this section of the book. Many children learn to add, subtract, multiply, and divide, but never understand the interrelationships between these processes.

The following activities utilize some basic computational skills, but require the learner to apply these skills to situations and experiences that might be faced in our world today. These experiences include the ability to make change; to apply the concept of time; to hypothesize about length and height; to plan and make purchases based on a budget; and even to maintain a checking account.

Also included in this section are opportunities for the children to utilize their logical reasoning abilities and strengthen their problem-solving skills through many activities, from collecting and analyzing survey results to interpreting and analyzing number patterns. The children are given many opportunities to solve real-life word problems, too.

WHAT COMES NEXT

Patterning is a skill that is very difficult for most children; however, the bright student thrives on trying to solve a problem logically. Very young children appear to have a natural ability that often is not developed. The best way to begin the teaching of patterning is by using a group of objects. At first, be sure to use objects that differ in only one way, such as color, shape, or size. Some examples appear here.

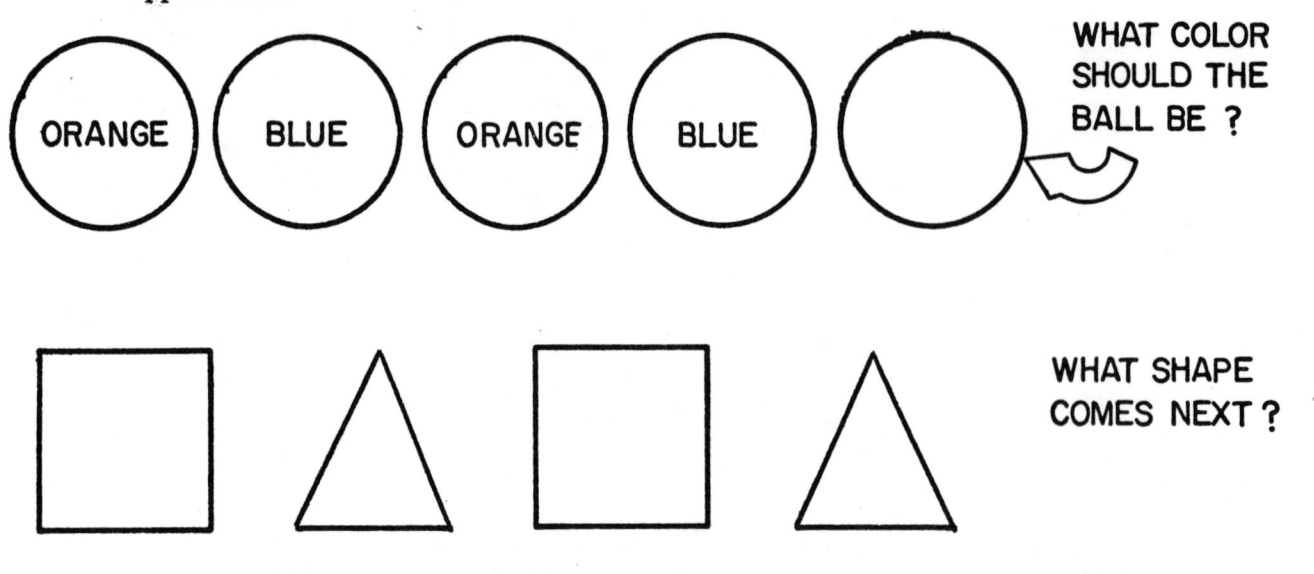

ORANGE   BLUE   ORANGE   BLUE

WHAT COLOR SHOULD THE BALL BE?

WHAT SHAPE COMES NEXT?

The children should be given the opportunity to make patterns for each other and handle the objects. After much practice, the children can complete the patterning activity sheets beginning on page 47. Observing individual students will help you identify which students are ready to move on.

Name _____ Date _____

What's Next ?

Directions: Draw the object that would come next in the box.

1. 
2. 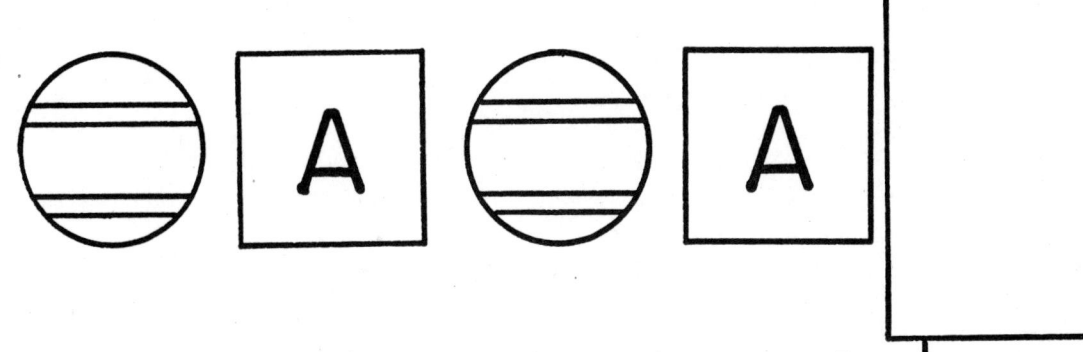
3. 
4.

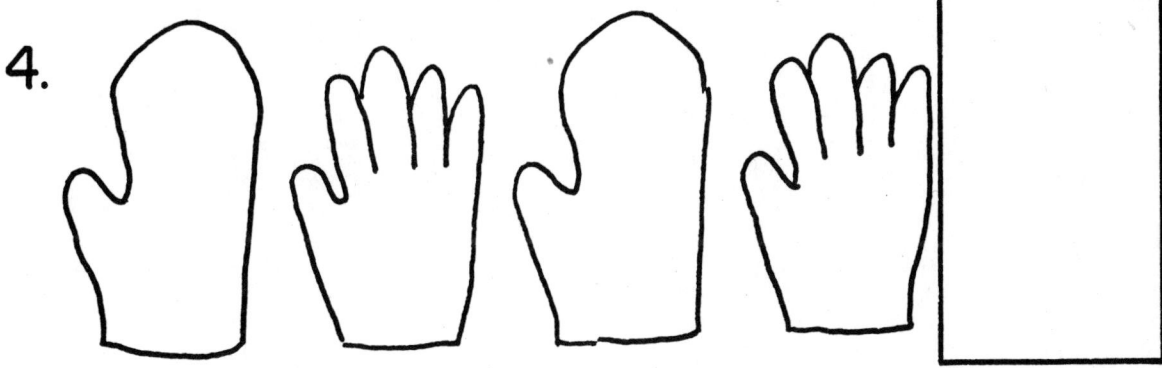

47

Name _____ Date _____

Fruity Line-Up!

Directions: Draw the next two pictures in line.

1. 
2. 
3. 
4. 
5.

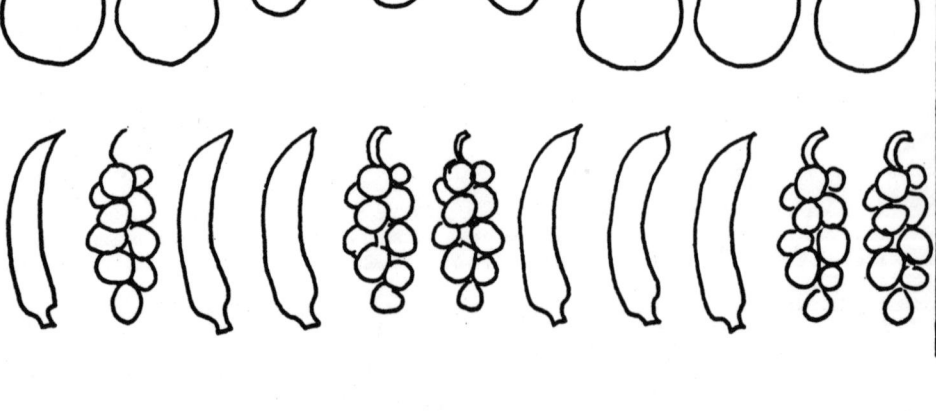

© 1985 by The Center for Applied Research in Education, Inc.

48

Name _____ Date _____

Next in Line !

Directions: Draw the next object in line in the box.

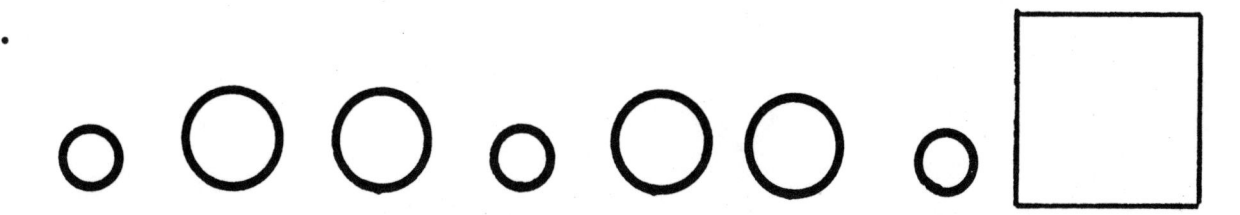

1.

2. A a a A a a A a

3.

4.

© 1985 by The Center for Applied Research in Education, Inc.

49

Name _____ Date _____

Number Line-Up!

Directions: Write the next number in the box.

1. 2 2 1 1 2 2 1 1 2 ☐

2. 8 8 8 8 8 8 8 8 8 8 8 8 ☐

3. 6 6 7 7 8 8 9 9 10 ☐

4. 3 3 5 5 7 7 9 ☐

5. 4 4 6 6 8 8 10 10 ☐

Name _____ Date _____

The Number Train I

Directions: Write the numbers that follow on the line.

1. 234, 345, 456, ___ ___ ___

2. 56 56 67 67 78 78 ___ ___ ___

3. 9 8 87 76 65 ___ ___ ___

4. 1, 4, 7, 10, 13, 16, ___ ___ ___

5. 35, 30, 25, 20, 15, ___ ___ ___

6. 30, 28, 26, 24, 22, ___ ___ ___

Name _____ Date _____

The Number Train II

Directions: Make up your own number patterns and put the correct answers on the back. Trade with a friend.

1.

2.

3.

4.

5.

Name _____ Date _____

The Line-Up !

Directions: Make up your own pattern. Put the correct answers on the back. Trade with a friend.

1.

2.

3.

4.

5.

6.

BIG BIG BRONTOSAURUS

While studying about dinosaurs, have the children decide which of these giants was the biggest. Do they really have any idea how long 70 feet is? Do they really know how tall 30-35 feet is? To make these sizes more meaningful, you may want to try this project on measurement.

On the playground, the children should measure off 70 feet using string. Now measure off 30 feet for the height of the dinosaur. This will help the children understand the size of these ancient reptiles. If you have some time available for marking ball fields, use white flour to draw the outline of the dinosaur for a clear picture of what it would look like.

This activity can be extended to include scale, such as one inch is equal to one foot (1″ = 1′). How many inches long would the dinosaur be? How many inches high? Now make this dinosaur out of cardboard using these scales. For example:

$$70 \text{ feet} = 70 \text{ inches}$$
$$35 \text{ feet} = 35 \text{ inches}$$

The dinosaur would be 70 inches long and 35 inches high.

Name _____   Date _____

Coats of Many Colors

Directions: Read the story problem. Answer the questions.

In the coat closet there were three coats—a red, a blue, and a green one. John's coat was red, Jim's coat had a zipper, and Jean's coat had a missing button. Jim did not like the color blue, and Jean only liked coats with pockets.

What color is Jim's coat? _____

What color is Jean's coat? _____

What color coat has pockets? _____

What color coat has a zipper? _____

55

Name _____   Date _____

Shoe Power

Directions: Read the word problem and write the answer on the blank.

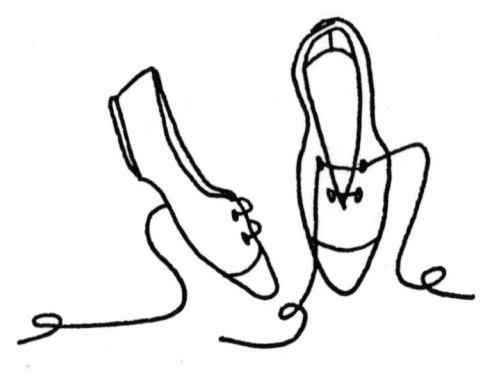

Jill had two red toe shoes and four black toe shoes. How many pairs of toe shoes did she have in all? _____

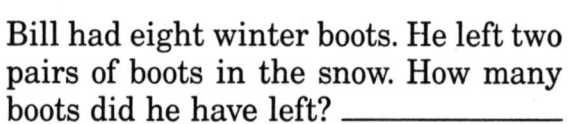

Bill had eight winter boots. He left two pairs of boots in the snow. How many boots did he have left? _____

Tom had four pairs of flip-flops. How many single flip-flops is that all together? _____

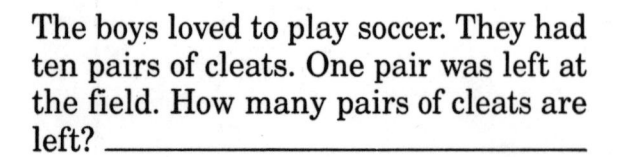

The boys loved to play soccer. They had ten pairs of cleats. One pair was left at the field. How many pairs of cleats are left? _____

56

Name _____   Date _____

SWEET TREATS

I want to buy	They cost	I have	I need
🍭🍭🍭🍭🍭🍭🍭	¢	8¢	¢
🍭🍭🍭🍭🍭🍭🍭🍭	¢	3¢	¢
🍭🍭🍭	¢	0¢	¢
🍭🍭🍭🍭🍭	¢	6¢	¢
🍭🍭🍭🍭🍭🍭🍭	¢	10¢	¢
🍭🍭🍭🍭🍭🍭🍭🍭 🍭🍭🍭🍭🍭	¢	13¢	¢

Name _____   Date _____

MAKING CHANGE

	TOTAL	SPENT	LEFT
25¢ 1¢ 1¢ 1¢ 1¢ 5¢	¢	30¢	¢
1¢ 1¢ 1¢ 25¢ 10¢ 10¢ 10¢	¢	40¢	¢
5¢ 5¢ 5¢ 5¢ 25¢ 1¢	¢	22¢	¢
10¢ 10¢ 25¢ 5¢ 5¢ 1¢ 1¢	¢	27¢	¢
1¢ 1¢ 1¢ 1¢ 1¢ 5¢ 5¢ 10¢	¢	23¢	¢
25¢ 25¢ 1¢ 1¢ 1¢ 1¢ 5¢	¢	43¢	¢
5¢ 5¢ 5¢ 25¢ 10¢ 10¢ 1¢	¢	50¢	¢

© 1985 by The Center for Applied Research in Education, Inc.

Name _____   Date _____

USE YOUR HEAD, then USE YOUR CALCULATOR

Coins	Total	Spent	Left	Calculator Check
25 25 25 10 10 5	¢	17¢	¢	¢
10 10 10 25 5 5 1	¢	18¢	¢	¢
5 5 5 25 1 1 1	¢	25¢	¢	¢
10 10 10 5 5 1 1	¢	20¢	¢	¢
5 5 5 5 1 1 1 1	¢	15¢	¢	¢
25 10 10 10 10 5 1 1	¢	50¢	¢	¢
25 25 5 5 1 1 1	¢	19¢	¢	¢

TIMELY MATH

I left home	I arrived at Grandma's	I left Grandma's	I arrived at home	I was gone?
2:00	2:30	2:45	3:00	____ hours and ____ minutes
				____ hours and ____ minutes
				____ hours and ____ minutes
				____ hours and ____ minutes
				____ hours and ____ minutes

© 1985 by The Center for Applied Research in Education, Inc.

Name _____ Date _____

MINUTE BY MINUTE

I left home.	I arrived.	It took how long?
2:00	4:00	_____ minutes
		_____ minutes
		_____ minutes
		_____ minutes
		_____ minutes

61

WHAT'S FOR DINNER?

When studying money or nutrition, help your group of students plan a menu using food advertisements from the local newspaper. Plan one as a group to give them the idea of how to do it. They need to choose foods from the correct food groups to make a balanced meal. (A balanced meal needs an item from each of the four basic food groups.) The specific advertisements should be cut out and pasted in a column so a total can be reached. For example:

Broccoli 39¢	....	.39
Steak $1.49	....	1.49
Potatoes 40¢	....	.40
Bread 98¢	....	.98
Milk $1.50	....	1.50
		$4.76

Now have the students plan a "Super Dinner" that contains five things that they would *really* like to eat if they could buy anything they wanted. Have each child cut out his or her choices from the newspaper ads and paste them onto large sheets of construction paper. If they cannot find an ad for an item they would like, have them make an ad for it and give it a price that they think is reasonable. For example:

Ice cream 46¢	....	.46
Cake 30¢	....	.30
Soda 40¢	....	.40
Chips 80¢	....	.80
Candy 67¢	....	.67
		$2.63

The students must then total the cost of their items correctly.

There are many other activities that can be done using the newspaper ads when studying money, such as planning a classroom party, buying a special book, or spending a Saturday afternoon at the movies. Try putting limits on what can be spent. Tell the children that they have to purchase items totaling a specific amount ($3.59). You may want to use the following activity sheets with young children. The sky's the limit. Use your imagination.

Name _____ Date _____

SHOPPING AT THE SCHOOL STORE

Directions: Circle the school supplies that you could purchase if you had $1.27.

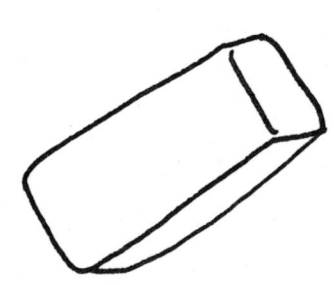

PENCIL – 10¢

ERASER – 12¢

NOTEBOOKS – 55¢

FOLDER – 25¢

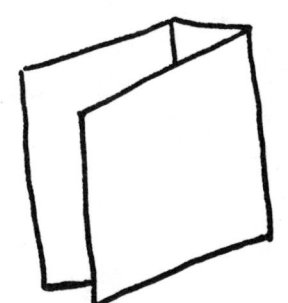

PEN – 30¢

BOOKCOVER – 50¢

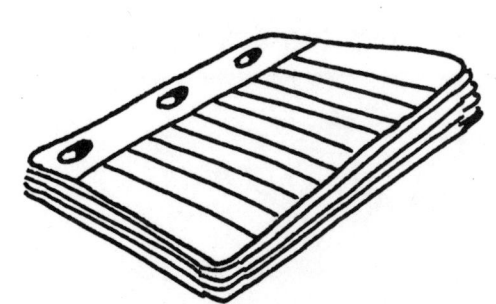

PACK OF PAPER – 25¢

PENCIL ERASER – 5¢

63

Name _____ Date _____

Christmas Wish List

Directions: You have $2.00 to spend at a toy store. Cut out the pictures of toys you can buy.

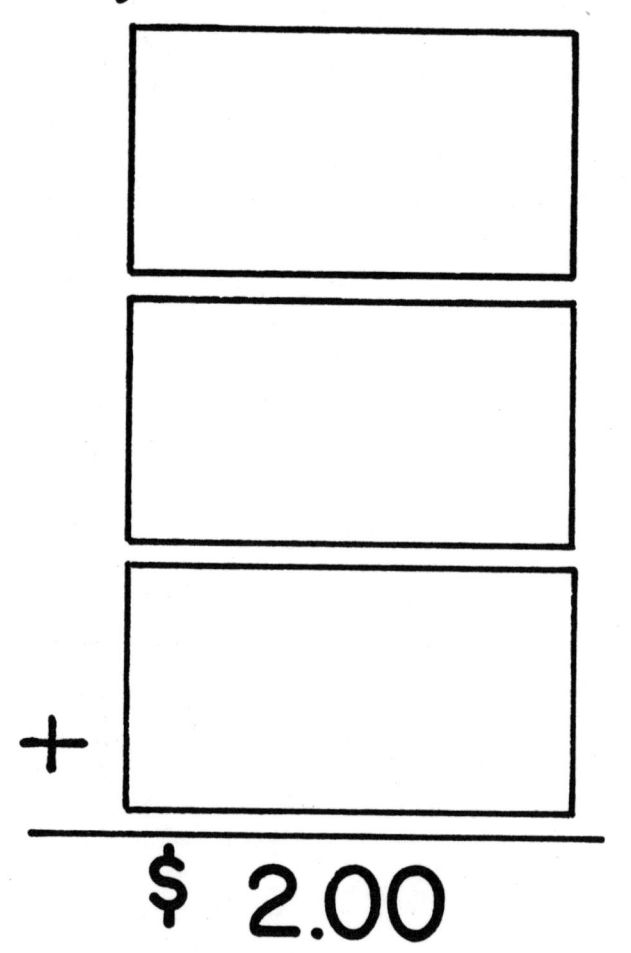

```
+ [      ]
  [      ]
  [      ]
  _____
  $ 2.00
```

price tag 50¢

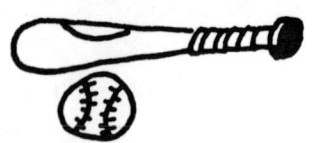

price tag 50¢

price tag 75¢

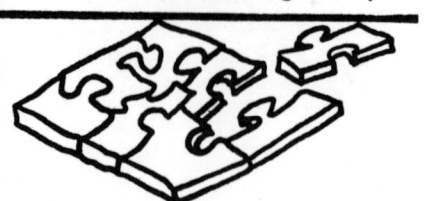

price tag 25¢

price tag $1.00

price tag 25¢

price tag 25¢

© 1985 by The Center for Applied Research in Education, Inc.

64

Clock Puzzlers

Tom has a cuckoo clock. It is not working properly. Tom has noticed that it cuckooed at 9:30 A.M., 12:30 P.M., and 3:30 P.M. Tom wants to take a nap. It is about 5:00 P.M. At what time can Tom expect the clock to cuckoo and wake him up? _____

How many times will the clock cuckoo between 5:00 P.M. and 12:00 midnight? List the times below.

_____

Name _____ Date _____

TIME OUT!

Directions: Find the answers to each of the word problems below.

1. Billy and Susie ride the bus home from school each day. On Wednesday afternoon, Billy and Susie got off the bus at 3:15 P.M. They both knew that there were two ways to get home. If they took the shortcut through some friends' backyards, they could be home in 20 minutes. If they walked home by the road, the walk would take 25 minutes. If Billy and Susie decide to take the shortcut, what time will they arrive home? Place an orange X on the correct clock. If they walked along the road, what time would they arrive home? Place a blue circle around the correct clock.

2. On school nights Susie goes to bed at 8:45 P.M. Thursday night was a school night, but she wanted to finish watching a TV special. It was to be over 15 minutes past her usual bedtime. At what time did Susie go to bed? _____
Susie gets up at 7:15 A.M. every morning to get ready for school. How much sleep did Susie get on Thursday night? Use the clock to help you figure out the answer.

3. Billy loves to take a bath. He has many toys to play with in the bathtub. Each night he has a 20-minute limit on his bath time because he takes up so much time in the bathroom and his sister Susie needs a bath, too. During a school week, if Billy takes a bath every night, how many minutes does he spend in the bath? _____
Hours? _____

66

Egg-citing Survey

Discuss taking a survey with the students in your classroom. Talk about the many different kinds of surveys and how survey information is used to draw conclusions about a particular issue or event. Then have the children collect some survey information on their own. Be sure to begin with a familiar topic.

After a brainstorming session about the many different ways eggs can be cooked and served, follow these simple steps to conduct a survey.

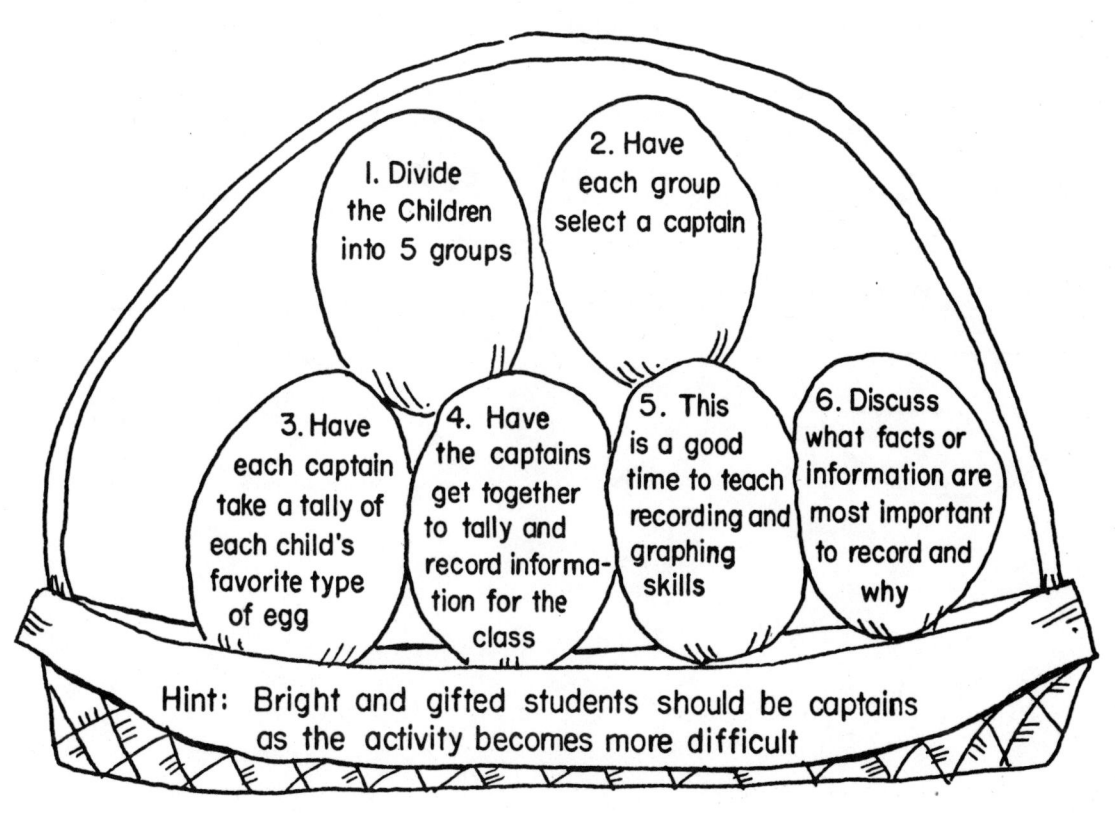

1. Divide the Children into 5 groups

2. Have each group select a captain

3. Have each captain take a tally of each child's favorite type of egg

4. Have the captains get together to tally and record information for the class

5. This is a good time to teach recording and graphing skills

6. Discuss what facts or information are most important to record and why

Hint: Bright and gifted students should be captains as the activity becomes more difficult

After the egg information has been recorded, discuss the findings with the group. From the findings see if the children can write the answers to the following questions and fill the basket on page 69 with these eggs.
(You can use the back of the egg for your explanation.)

How many girls liked Scrambled eggs? _____
Boys? _____

What is the favorite type of egg for the girls? _____
Boys? _____

If you were going to fix eggs for our class, what kind would you fix and why? _____ _____ _____

What do you think would be the favorite kind of egg for all boys and girls your age and why? _____ _____

How many girls liked Scrambled eggs and Boiled eggs? _____
Boys? _____

What kind of eggs do you think most girls like? _____ _____
Why? _____ _____
Boys? _____ _____

Name _____ Date _____

BANKING IS MY BUSINESS

Children have been fascinated with money from the time they were toddlers. Their parents and grandparents have probably given them money to place in a piggy bank, but few children have had the opportunity to take their money to a bank or to find out how a bank and banker can be helpful.

Discuss with the children the importance of a banker in their community. Talk about the different ways a banker can help them—saving money, lending money, maintaining a checking account, etc. After you discuss all of the activities that take place at a bank, have the children try to complete the following banking activity sheets. You may want to get sample checks from a local bank and let the children write "real" checks!

Name _____   Date _____

HAVING YOUR OWN CHECKING ACCOUNT

Directions: Examine the sample check below and note all of its parts. Now write your own checks for the items indicated.

Name, Address, Phone Number   Check Number

Jason P. Smith
1324 Holly Berry Court   374
Belmont, Virginia 22136
PH 689-3101   January 1, 1984 ← Date

PAY TO THE
ORDER OF _____Johnson Cleaners_____ $ 10.98 ← Amount of Check

_____Ten dollars and 98/100--------------------------------DOLLARS ←

Savings & Money
National Bank

Memo ____Cleaning_____   *Jason P. Smith*

1: 0689   7007382   6321   0470   0221

What money is   Bank Number   Signature
spent for   Checking Account Number

71

Name _____   Date _____

1. Write a check for $3.51 to Skinner's Toys. Be sure to include all parts of a check.

```
  _____
  _____
  _____                                        _____ 19_____
  _____
  PAY TO THE
  ORDER OF _____ . $_____
            _____ DOLLARS
              Savings & Money
              National Bank
  Memo _____   _____
  1: 0689   7007382   6321   0470   0221
```

2. Write a check for $1925.00 for a new Apple IIE Computer purchased from Computer Gadgets.

```
  _____
  _____
  _____                                        _____ 19_____
  _____
  PAY TO THE
  ORDER OF _____ . $_____
            _____ DOLLARS
              Savings & Money
              National Bank
  Memo _____   _____
  1: 0689   7007382   6321   0470   0221
```

Name _____   Date _____

BALANCING MY OWN CHECKBOOK

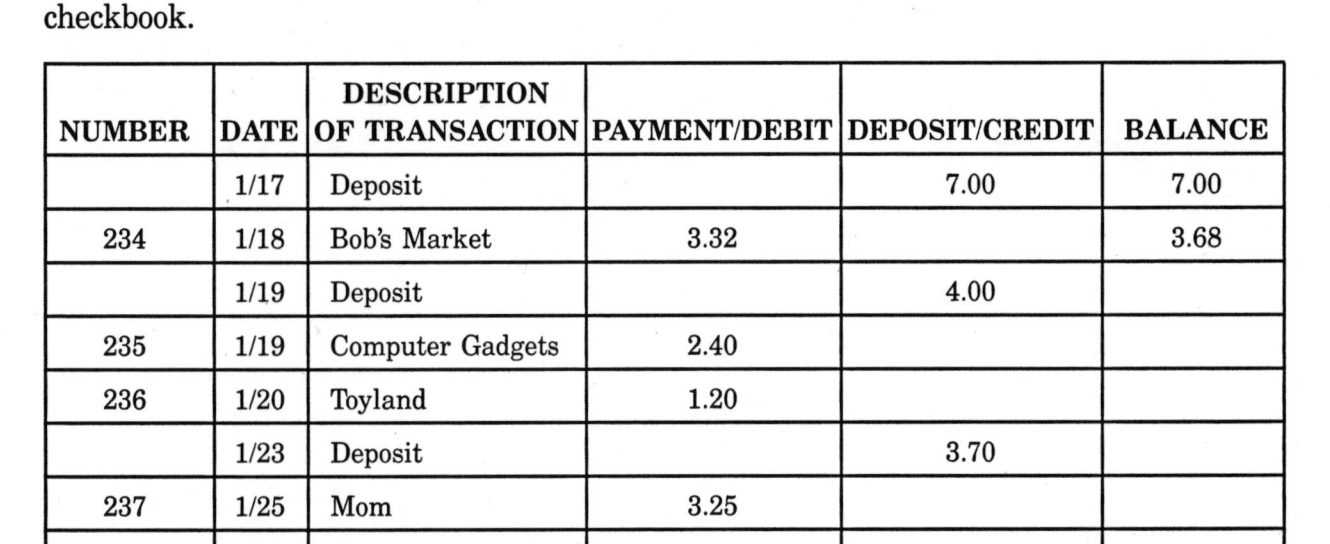

Directions: Using the amounts of money given, keep a running balance of your own checkbook.

NUMBER	DATE	DESCRIPTION OF TRANSACTION	PAYMENT/DEBIT	DEPOSIT/CREDIT	BALANCE
	1/17	Deposit		7.00	7.00
234	1/18	Bob's Market	3.32		3.68
	1/19	Deposit		4.00	
235	1/19	Computer Gadgets	2.40		
236	1/20	Toyland	1.20		
	1/23	Deposit		3.70	
237	1/25	Mom	3.25		
238	1/25	Ginny's Jeans	2.27		

Name _____ Date _____

BORROWING MONEY

Directions: Read the following problems and write the answers to each in the box provided.

1. For the privilege of borrowing money, you must pay interest. Tom wants to borrow $10.00 from the bank to buy a new horn for his bike. He will have to pay $1.10 each month for 10 months to pay back what he borrowed. Tom paid ☐ in interest.

2. Sally wants to buy a new computer. She can purchase one for $1500.00 Her father said that he would pay the $1500.00 if she would pay the interest on the loan. They will have to pay $165.00 for 10 months to pay back the loan. Sally will pay ☐ in interest.

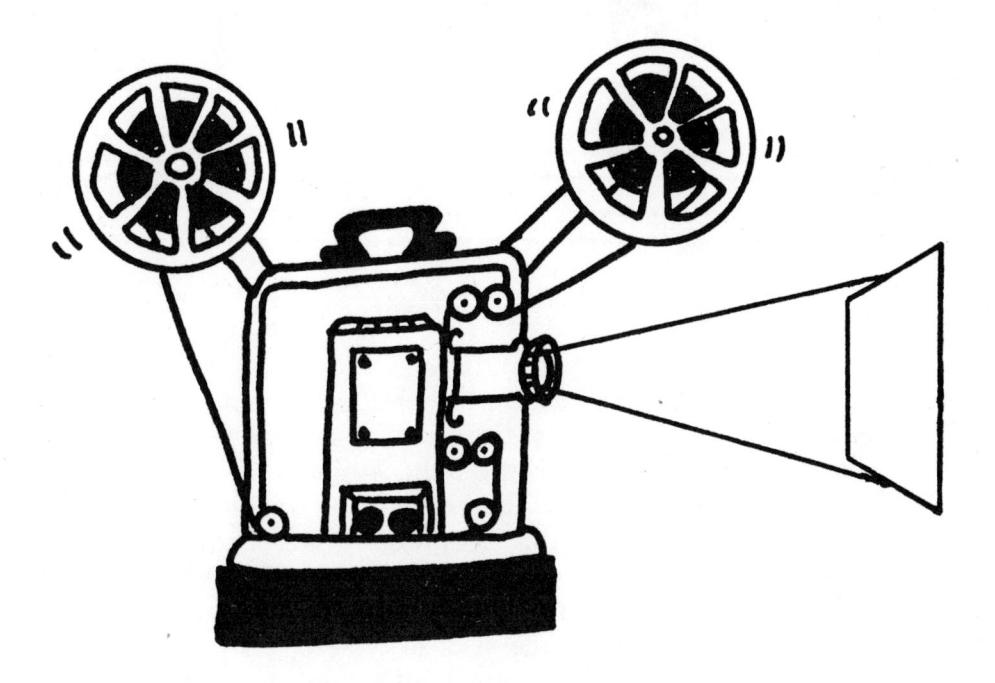

SECTION III
TURN ON WITH
SOCIAL STUDIES

Developing and understanding concepts are the main focus of the social studies section of this book. Rather than encouraging an accumulation of factual information, it is important that gifted students be given opportunities to take facts, apply them, and draw conclusions.

Within this section are many opportunities for the children to explore the community and the world around them. They can begin their study with a re-creation of yesterday by becoming active participants in an archaeological dig. There are opportunities to find hidden treasures by developing and utilizing their map skills and they can even trace their own family history and create their family tree.

Also included are opportunities for the children to use both inductive and deductive reasoning. They are encouraged to explore various forms of communication from body language to Braille. They are then given the opportunity to communicate to the world by creating their own newspaper.

WHAT'S INSIDE?

Change is a very difficult concept for children to understand. There is no better way for children to discover how change occurs than by using changes in themselves (their height, weight, shoe size, etc.).

Have the children create a time capsule at the beginning of the school year and include anything they would like about themselves, their families, their experiences. For some students this may be enough direction; for others you may need to provide some suggestions (a picture of themselves, their shoe size, lost teeth, etc.). Perhaps you would like to have the children complete the "All About Me" activity sheet on page 77 to include in their time capsule. After the children have gathered the information, objects, and materials that they would like to include, place them in a jar. A large plastic mayonnaise jar from a restaurant will hold all the entries. Then, bury them someplace in the school yard.

At the end of the school year, have the children complete the activity sheet again. Then go to the school yard and dig up the time capsule. The children will be surprised to find out how much they have changed since the beginning of the school year. You should encourage the children to take their time capsules home and bury them for five years. You will have lots of surprise visitors when they find their treasure buried in the years to come. Many students will come back to visit you, just to comment on how they have changed. What a super way to remember and understand change!

ALL ABOUT ME

_____ Date

My name is _____.

I am ___ years old. My birthday is _____.

I weigh ___ pounds, am ___ tall, and wear a size ___ shoe.

I have ___ teeth missing.

My favorite TV show or commercial is _____.

I like to eat _____.

I like to _____ after school each day.

My favorite book is _____

and my favorite subject in school is _____.

The best vacation that I ever had was when _____
_____.

I would like to grow up to be _____.

The last movie I saw was _____.

This is my picture:

© 1985 by The Center for Applied Research in Education, Inc.

I WANT TO KNOW ABOUT ME!

```
GRANDPA  GRANDMA      GRANDPA  GRANDMA
    └────┬────┘          └────┬────┘
      FATHER                MOTHER
         └──────────┬──────────┘
                   ME
```

    When children first come to school, they usually know about their immediate families. This is an excellent opportunity to gather additional information about their families and to take a look at old family albums and pictures. Ask the parents to help their children write the information on the "My Family Tree" activity sheet on page 79 to insure that the names are spelled correctly. Have the children gather information about the members of their families to share with the class. Have each child make a presentation to the class about his or her family history and some unusual experiences that might be of interest. This is an excellent way to involve the parents, step-parents, guardians, and grandparents. Perhaps students can bring some family members to class with them on their presentation day.

MY FAMILY TREE

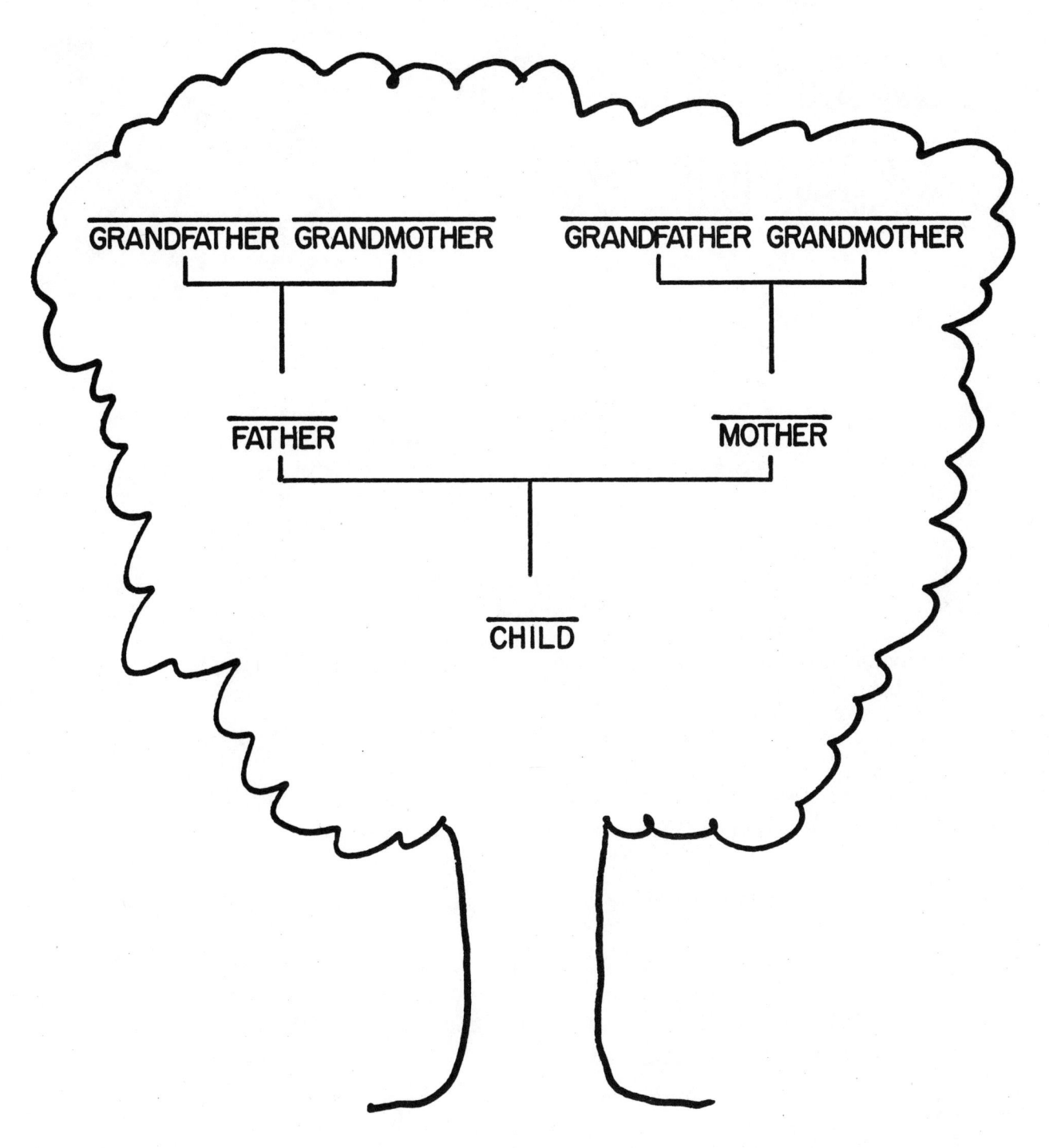

GRANDFATHER GRANDMOTHER   GRANDFATHER GRANDMOTHER

FATHER   MOTHER

CHILD

© 1985 by The Center for Applied Research in Education, Inc.

I WANT TO KNOW ABOUT YOU!

Oral history is an interesting way of preserving the past. This can be an exciting project for your verbal students. You will need a tape recorder and a list of questions. It is a good idea to have students practice with each other before interviewing grandparents, an aunt, an uncle, or some older person in the community. Parents may want to supplement the questions with ones appropriate for the particular person being interviewed.

When the student begins a taping session, he or she should begin by identifying him- or herself, the person with whom he or she is speaking, and the date. It is a good idea to have some questions on 3" × 5" cards so that the child can cover the point he or she wants to find out about. Here are some good questions to get the child started.

1. "When you were growing up, what kinds of games did you play?"
2. "What else did you do for fun?"
3. "What was your day like when you were in elementary school?"
4. "What was your favorite subject? Why did you like it?"
5. "Tell me about the clothes you wore. Were there any unusual styles?"
6. "Tell me about the home you lived in. How was it different from the one you live in today?"
7. "Do you have any toys, clothing, pictures, or special things you saved from childhood? Would you tell me about them and why you saved them?"
8. "Tell me about your favorite holiday and how you celebrated it."
9. "Would you come to school and share these things with my class?"

As a follow-up to the activity, the children may want to keep a scrapbook of information that can be passed on to their own children and grandchildren. Some things that would be good to include are photographs at holiday times, photos that show clothing style, and even pictures of the inside and outside of their houses. Besides photos, students can include newspaper headlines, party invitations, samples of school work, names of teachers and friends, and lists of their favorite things from games to toothpaste brands.

WHERE AM I?

Making maps requires a lot of abstract reasoning ability, a characteristic that is generally evident in the young bright child. To introduce your children to map making, take a few children on a short walk through the school building. Be sure to encourage the children to observe carefully as they begin their walk. Draw a map on a large sheet of chart paper, and indicate the route you have taken from the classroom to the office, cafeteria, library, etc., and back to the classroom. Explain the importance of landmarks. When you get back to the classroom, take several new children on your trip and see if they can follow the map that the earlier group made. This will help the children to understand the importance of accuracy in map making. Whenever there is confusion, have the original map makers add to their map to make it clearer and easier to understand.

After this orientation, the students will be ready to try their hand at their own map making.

Give each child paper and pencil and take them on a walk around the school grounds or the block near your school. Ask them to draw their maps as you go. When you return to the classroom, draw a map on the board or sheet of chart paper for comparison.

Discuss with the children similarities and differences between your map and their maps. You may even have to verify some points on the map. Talk about the difficulty of map making and its importance. Make a list on a chart of all of the people who use maps. Here is a sample.

People Who Use Maps

1. Truckers
2. Pilots
3. Automobile Drivers
4. Oceanographers
5. Mountain Climbers
6. Forest Rangers
7. Real Estate Developers
8. Sailors

You should also discuss with the children the many different kinds of maps; make a list of these, too. Have the children collect as many types of maps as they can find. They can write letters to several resource people for copies of such maps as aerial maps and oceanographic maps. You may also want to invite a cartographer to visit the classroom to talk to the children.

COMMUNICATION

A bulletin board can be an excellent tool to stimulate creative thinking. Using an opaque projector, enlarge the bulletin board illustration on page 83 to illustrate various ways of communicating.

Discuss the various methods of communicating with the children. After the discussion is completed, ask your students if they can think of other ways people communicate. Make a chart of all the ways they can think of. Be sure that they include communication techniques of people with special needs, such as the blind, deaf, etc. This is also the time to discuss some of the special needs that these groups of people may have. You may want to invite a resource person into your room who can share an unusual form of communication, such as Braille or sign language. You may then have the children complete one or more of the communication activity sheets that follow in this section. Encourage the children to use all of their resources—the library, special agencies, doctors, friends, etc. Be sure that you schedule time for the children to share.

How Communication Has Changed

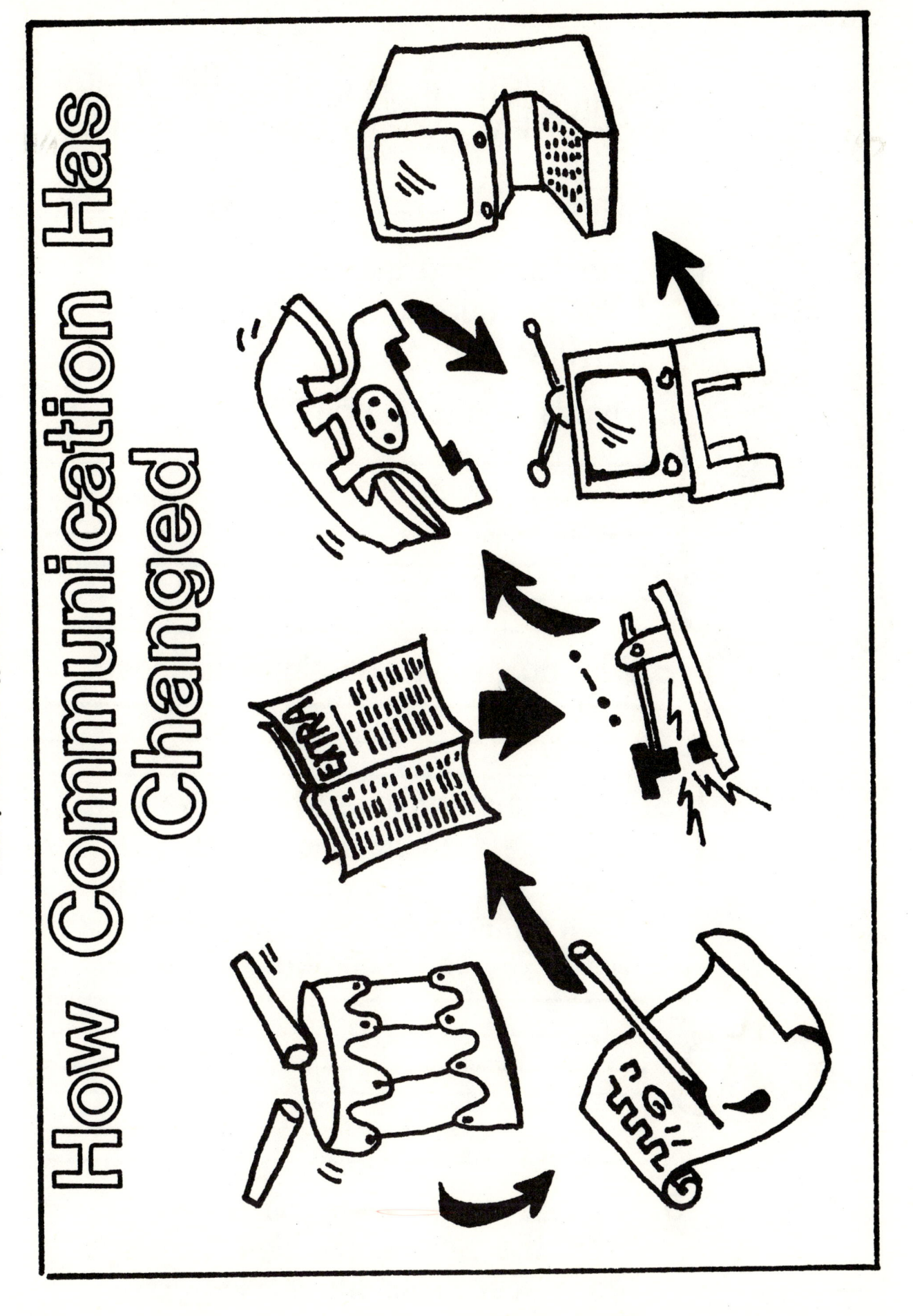

Name _____ Date _____

SIGN LANGUAGE

Name _____ Date _____

Directions: Find the answers to the following questions or complete the activities.

1. What is sign language?
   _____
   _____
   _____
   _____

2. Why do people use sign language?
   _____
   _____

3. Do you know anyone who knows sign language? Circle one. YES NO

4. Using a book or a resource person learn some sign language. Write the words you can sign here.
   _____
   _____
   _____
   _____

5. Now tell your teacher you are ready to tell the class about sign language. Teach your class the signing you have learned.

© 1985 by The Center for Applied Research in Education, Inc.

BODY LANGUAGE

Name _____ Date _____

Directions: Find the answers to the following questions or complete the activities.

1. What are some ways that we use our bodies to tell people how we feel about them?
   _____
   _____
   _____
   _____

2. What is communicated by each of the faces below? Select one of these words and write it below each face.

SAD   ANGRY   HAPPY

_____   _____   _____
_____   _____   _____

85

3. How do you show you are happy with your body?
_____
- - - - - - - - - - - - - - - - - -
_____

Show that you are sad?
_____
- - - - - - - - - - - - - - - - - -
_____

4. Is your face the only part of the body that communicates how you feel?

   Circle one. YES NO

5. What other ways do you communicate with your body?
_____
- - - - - - - - - - - - - - - - - -
_____
- - - - - - - - - - - - - - - - - -
_____

6. What are some ways your teacher shows that he or she is happy?
_____
- - - - - - - - - - - - - - - - - -
_____

Shows that he or she is disappointed?
_____
- - - - - - - - - - - - - - - - - -
_____

Social Studies: relating and interpreting

© 1985 by The Center for Applied Research in Education, Inc.

BRAILLE

Name _____ Date _____

Directions: Find the answers to the following questions or complete the activities.

1. What is Braille?
   _____
   _____
   _____
   _____

2. Why do people use Braille?
   _____
   _____

3. Do you know anyone who knows how to read Braille? Circle one. Yes   No

4. Try to visit your public library and check out a Braille book to share with your classmates.

5. Using a book or a resource person learn to read some Braille words. Write down the alphabet in Braille. (Hint: Braille is based on a series of 6 dots ⠿) Use a resource book to find out more information.

FUTURE COMMUNICATION

Name _____ Date _____

Directions: Find the answers to the following questions or complete the activities.

1. Make a list of all of the ways that we communicate now.
   _____
   _____
   _____
   _____
   _____
   _____

2. For each of the ways you listed above think of a way that might be substituted and used in the future.
   _____
   _____
   _____
   _____
   _____
   _____

3. For what reasons may our ways of communication change?

_____
- - - - - - - - - - - - - - - - - -
_____
_____
- - - - - - - - - - - - - - - - - -
_____

4. Draw a picture of what you think our substitute telephone will look like.

A picture of our substitute television.

5. Imagine a machine that may be used to communicate 100 years from now. What do you think it will be able to do?

_____

- -

_____
_____

- -

_____

Draw a picture of your machine of the future.

EXTRA EXTRA
READ ALL ABOUT IT

Have the children bring in a newspaper from home. Discuss the parts of a newspaper (the front page news stories, editorials, advertisements, classified ads, sports, comics, etc.) with the children. During the discussion, allow time for each child to locate the parts discussed in his or her own newspaper.

Talk with the children about the importance of headlines. Talk about some catchy headlines that might be written about the well-known nursery rhyme, "Humpty Dumpty."

HUMPTY DUMPTY FALLS APART
ACCIDENT AT THE CASTLE
HUMPTY TAKES A GREAT FALL

Discuss why these headlines might attract readers. Then discuss some editorials, advertisements, or classified ads you might write about eggs to be included in your "Egghead Newspaper." Have each child select a section of "Egg News" to work on. When everyone has completed his or her section, collect and categorize them. Then have the children write their articles, etc., on adding machine tape. When the children have their articles completed and in final form, they can organize them and glue them in newspaper format onto large sheets of manila paper or newsprint. Don't forget to give your newspaper a name!

THE EGGHEAD PRESS

NUMBER 1

ACCIDENT AT THE CASTLE

CARY ELEMENTARY

EGGS FOR SALE
BEST PRICE IN TOWN!

COMICS

Bonjour! Buenos Dias!

Foreign languages fascinate young children and can stimulate an early interest in becoming articulate in a second language.

To prepare for this activity, write a simple phrase (e.g., a greeting) in several languages, each on a separate index card like the samples that follow:

Bonjour France	**guten Morgen** Germany
Buon Giorno Italy	**Buenos Dias** Spain

You may want to write the name of the country, too. You will need one card for each child in your group. After introducing the words on the cards and their meanings, explain to the children that you would like them to collect as much information as possible about their country, as well as other phrases in the language. They can go to the library, talk with friends and parents, or use any other sources they can think of. You may want to provide several parent-helpers to assist the children in collecting their information. It may be helpful to use the "Tidbits About" activity sheet on page 95 to help the children organize their information.

After the children have collected the information, the parent aides should help them put together a small presentation about their country. This presentation should integrate all the information they have collected as well as the phrases or words they have learned. Here is an example:

"Bonjour."
I have the country of France. When children go to school in France, they write on "papier" the same way we do. When they speak of their mother, they say...

Each child may want to make a prop to use during the presentation, such as a poster, chart, transparency, etc., or may enjoy dressing in the native dress of the country he or she is going to talk about. When the presentations are ready, the children should be given adequate time to share them with the class.

TID BITS ABOUT

_____
(NAME OF COUNTRY)

NAME _____ DATE _____

1. Location of my country –

2. Capital city – _____

3. Famous places –

4. Customs and dress –

© 1985 by The Center for Applied Research in Education, Inc.

5. Schools, children, games —

6. Foods —

7. Phrases and words to know —

8. Other interesting tidbits —

OLDIES BUT GOODIES

Many social studies units in the primary grades deal with the past. Children need to be taught about their heritage and ways to discover how old tools or instruments were used in daily life.

Create an interest center in your classroom that contains old household objects or tools (wooden churn, butter press, apple peeler, candle snuffer, and old bottles). Allow time for the center to generate a discussion among students. When the children begin asking about the objects or tools, it is time for a brainstorming session.

Discuss with the children possible uses of the object. Encourage the children to handle and experiment with the objects. You may have to supply the name of the object. Discuss how objects of today and yesterday are different and why.

Have the children bring old objects from home to share with the class. Allow time for them to explore individually before determining as a class the name and use of each object.

Children who have an interest and/or skill in solving problems such as the one above, should pursue the following career-related activity.

CAN YOU DIG IT?

Archaeologist: A person who digs up, puts into categories, and studies objects of ancient times whether they be people, customs, or tools.

Discuss with the children some of the great finds in archaeology—King Tut's tomb, dinosaur bones, and American Indian artifacts. Also talk about the duties of an archaeologist and the skills necessary to perform his or her job.

In order to allow the children an opportunity to experience the duties of an archaeologist, the following hands-on experience may be initiated.

Rope off an area outside large enough for the group of students to work in. Then place in the ground an old cup, saucer, and plate that has been broken into large pieces. (Preferably the dishes should be unmatched for easy identification later.) A diagram should be drawn to show where each piece has been buried. Be sure to place some pieces near the surface and others at varying levels. The diagram will ensure that all pieces have been found at the end of the excavation.

Before going outside to the site, discuss the following points with the children. (If a small group is participating, this can be done at recess time.)

1. What tools are needed—discuss the problem of using large tools and what they would do to the artifacts.
2. Collect tools—a bucket to move dirt, trowels, spoons, brushes, and cotton cloths.
3. Discuss how you go about digging up the objects—dangers of walking on the dig area, digging with force, and removing dirt improperly.
4. Mapping relative locations of finds as they are made.
5. Finding all the parts of the object—checking with the teacher to make sure that all pieces have been removed.

Take all the pieces of the "find" inside and brush and clean them carefully. Have the children put the pieces together. CLUE: The children should look at the pieces and categorize them according to their markings. For example: All flowered pieces go together, etc.

You may want to use modeling clay for sticking the pieces together until the children are sure that the parts fit correctly. After all objects are completed, they can be glued to their original shapes.

After completion, brainstorm with the group about how the archaeologist would find out about what the object was, what it was used for, or what it looked like. Consider the shape of the object, any writing or dates remaining on the object, the location of the find, and the past history of the people, customs, and animal life of the area. Consider how the object came to be in that particular place.

Then have the children complete the "Can You Dig It?" activity sheets on pages 100 and 101 about their finds and experiences as an archaeologist.

Name _____ Date _____

CAN YOU DIG IT?

Directions: Answer the following questions about your archaeological "find."

1. Circle the tools you used in the "dig."

   shovel   brushes   bulldozer   trowel   sifter

   spoon   rake   hoe   bucket

2. Circle the correct ways to remove objects from a "find."

   Dig with a big shovel.

   Remove a little dirt at a time.

   Jump on a "dig" area.

   Dig carefully with a spoon.

   Brush away dirt gently.

3. Underline the objects you found.

   shirt   cup   plate   sock

   house   saucer   horse   cow

4. List on the chart the clues you found for each object. (See the clues on the next page.)

Cup	Saucer	Plate

100

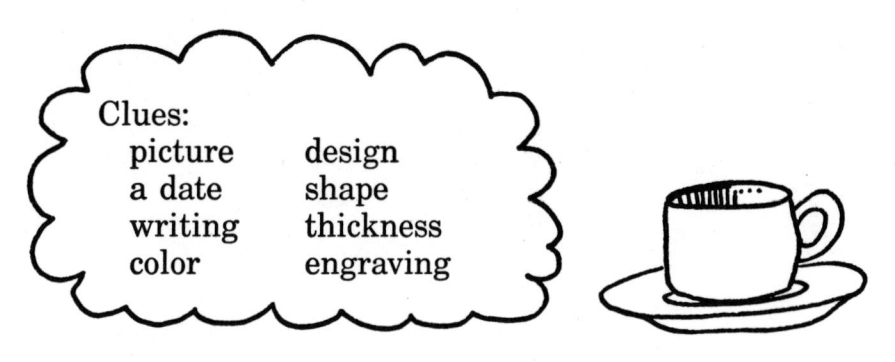

Clues:
- picture
- a date
- writing
- color
- design
- shape
- thickness
- engraving

5. Make a picture of what you found in the "dig."

6. Match the following words with their meanings.

   archaeologist   a place where objects are uncovered

   find   a tool for digging

   dig   an object found in a dig

   trowel   a person who digs up, puts into categories, and studies objects of ancient times

7. Put a check beside each task of an archaeologist.

   ___ Milks the cows

   ___ Removes dirt gently

   ___ Names the "find"

   ___ Plays ball on Saturday

   ___ Puts together the objects

   ___ Studies the past

   ___ Uses correct tools for digging

8. What did you like most about being an archaeologist? What did you like least?

101

SECTION IV

REALLY SHINE WITH SCIENCE

The science section of this book is geared to the exploring, questioning child who likes to hypothesize and make predictions. The specific activities are based on content found in most science programs. This enables you to provide appropriate extensions to the regular classroom curriculum.

The children are given many opportunities to observe and record information, from completing a weather chart to mapping information on a graph. They are also encouraged to hypothesize and draw conclusions about the information they have collected.

Many of the activities allow the children to utilize the tools of a scientist, from examining tiny creatures under the microscope to observing bird habits through binoculars.

Also included in this section is a career activity about the veterinarian. The children are given an opportunity to experience diagnosing an animal's problem and selecting a potential remedy.

ANIMALOLOGY!

When working on a unit on animals and their environment, it is exciting to encourage the children to create their own animal from several parts of animals. (See the parts on pages 105 and 106.) After arranging the "animal" on the paper, create the environment in which it is to live. Make sure the following questions are thought out and explained to the class:

1. Did you give the animal a food supply?
2. Is there a place to get water?
3. Is there enough room to exercise?
4. Is your animal protected (coloring, size, wings, etc.) from danger?
5. Does it have any predators?

105

106

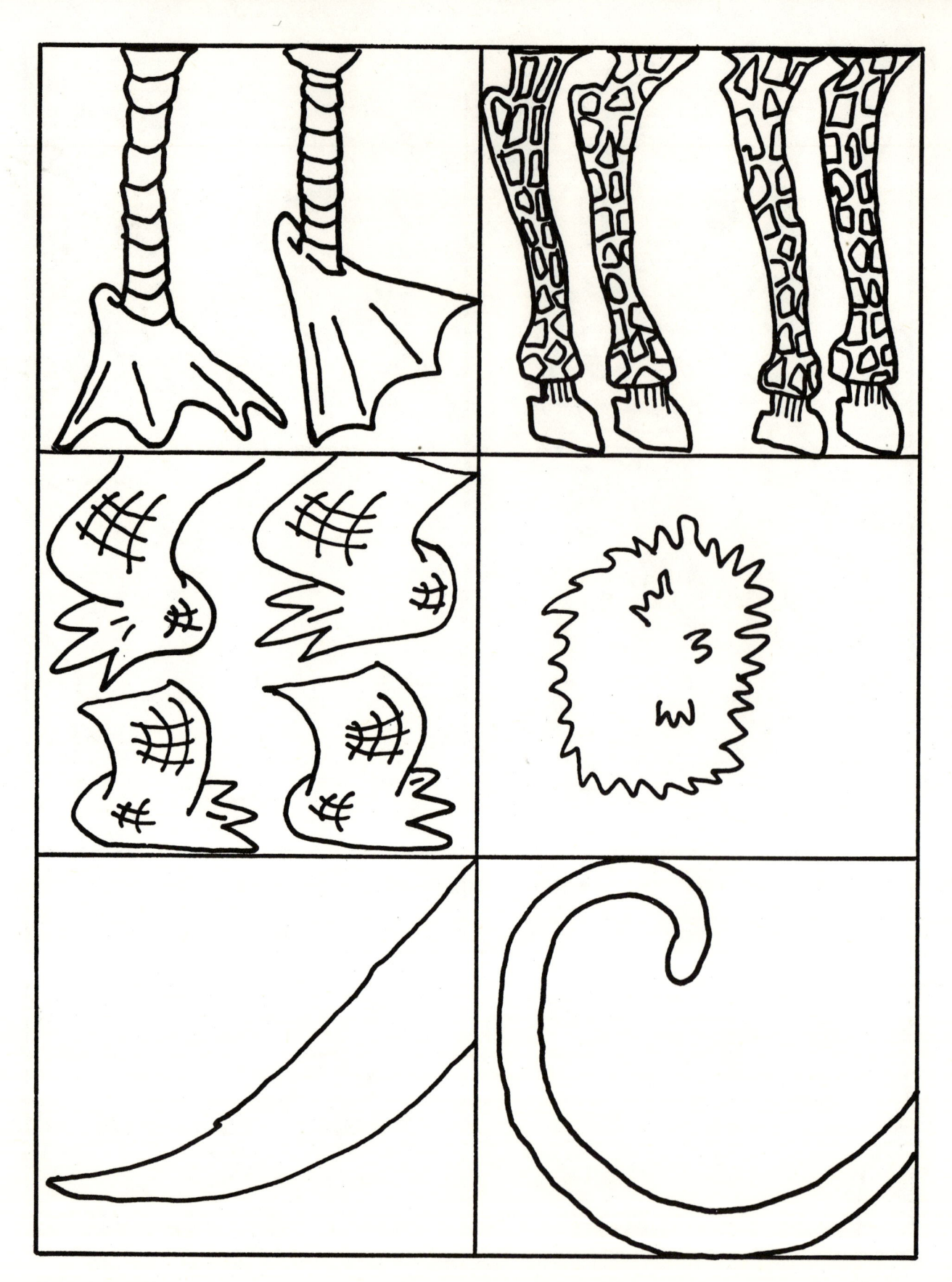

INSECTS

Bees, butterflies, and mosquitoes have characteristics in common. Do your students know what they are? Answers may be: they fly, they are small, or they are insects. When this fact is mentioned, have each child select a book about insects. After they have had a chance to browse through the books, make a group list of the characteristics of insects.

After you have made the list of characteristics, discuss the following questions with the children:

- How are these insects helpful? Harmful?
- What other kinds of insects can you think of? Are they helpful or harmful?
- If you could be any kind of insect, what insect would you want to be? Why?

After the discussion, have the children select an insect that they would like to act out silently. The other members of the group should try to decide which insect it is.

With your help or the help of an aide or volunteer parent, have the children choose one insect and develop a short play that depicts its good and bad habits. Students should make their own costumes and props for the play.

When they are ready, have the children perform for the class.

HEAR YE!
HEAR YE!

When you are working on a unit about sound, have the children make an old-fashioned telephone by connecting two empty cans with a long thick string.

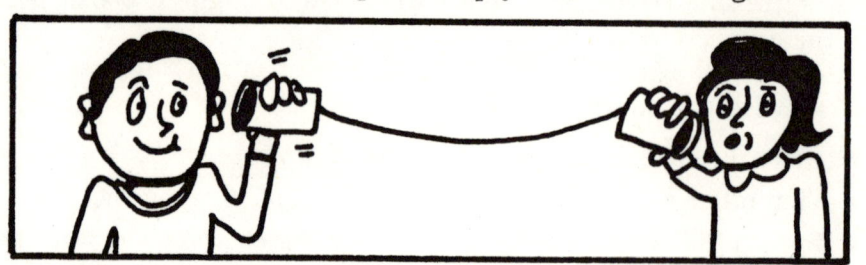

After allowing time for the children to talk to each other through the telephone, discuss some of the following questions:

1. Why do you think it is easier to hear your friend with the use of the "telephone"?
2. How did the sound of your voice travel to your friend?
3. What other materials make it easy for sound to travel?
4. If we were to set a ticking clock on these materials, which ones would sound loudest and which ones would sound softest? Why do you think this is so?
   a. wooden table   c. the ground   e. a pillow
   b. the floor   d. a book   f. an upside-down pot
5. Now try striking a triangle made of different materials with a metal dowel used for a musical triangle. Which made a louder sound? A softer sound? Why were some loud and some soft?
   Use triangles made of:
   a. metal   d. paper   f. sticks
   b. pipe cleaners e. a coat hanger g. rolled tin foil
   c. plastic

Now discuss with the children the difference between their homemade telephone and their telephone at home. Be sure to point out both similarities and differences.

The Wheel

When children think about machines, they often have a mental picture of a large complicated machine. Discussing a simple machine like the wheel and axle can help the child understand the very basic energy-saving devices.

You should begin with some basic questions:

1. What is a wheel?
2. Describe a wheel.
3. What would happen if a wheel had three sides? Four sides?
4. Do all wheels look alike?
5. What are some interesting wheels you've seen?

At the end of the day, give each child one of the questionnaires (see pages 110-113) to be taken home for a home project.

After the children have chosen and completed a home project, have them share it with the class.

This is a good time to set up a "Wheel Fun Center." Children could go to the center to work when they have extra time to create their own machines. Some supplies for the center could be:

spools	springs	pliers
sticks	rods (for axles)	wire
string	various wheels	small boards
cardboard	boxes	Tinkertoys
Rig-A-Jig	erector set	

Name _____   Date _____

Kitchen Wheels

1. Wheels in my kitchen are:

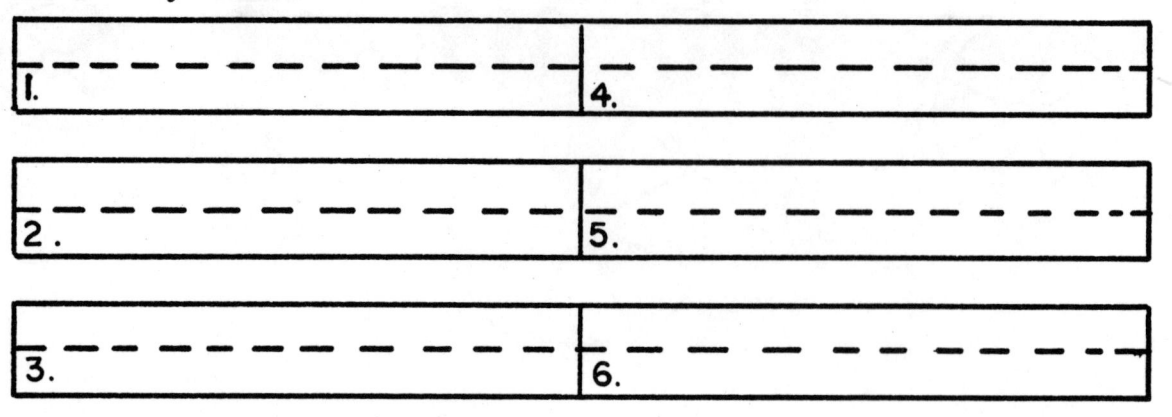

   | 1. | 4. |

   | 2. | 5. |

   | 3. | 6. |

2. The wheel I found most interesting was:

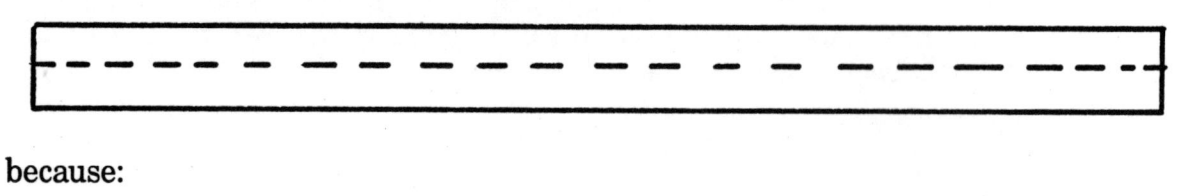

   because:

3. Here is a picture of the kitchen wheel I liked best.

4. Now draw or construct a wheel you might find in your kitchen in the year 2001.

© 1985 by The Center for Applied Research in Education, Inc.

110

Name _____ Date _____

Machines With One Wheel

1. Name some machines with one wheel.

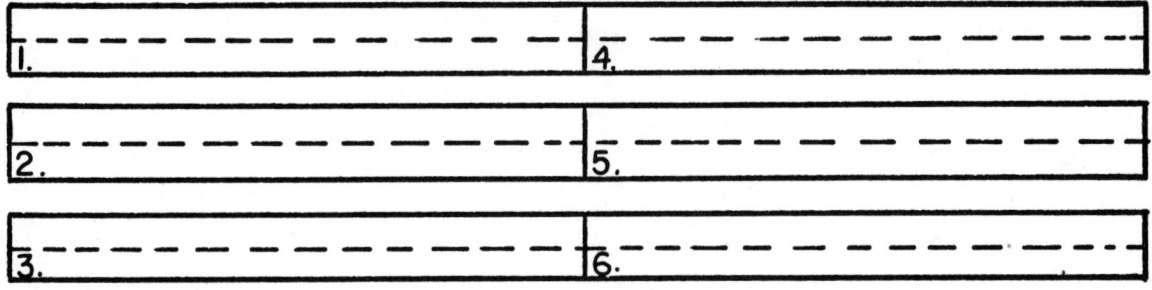

1. _____	4. _____
2. _____	5. _____
3. _____	6. _____

2. Draw a picture of a machine with one wheel.

3. Now draw a picture of a machine with one wheel that would be fun to ride.

4. If you could make a machine to ride 100 years from now, what would it look like? Make sure you give it only one wheel.

5. Now construct your project to share at school.

Name _____   Date _____

Three-Wheel Wonders

1. Draw pictures of three things that have three wheels.

①

② _____

③ _____

© 1985 by The Center for Applied Research in Education, Inc.

112

2. If you had three wheels and needed a machine to move some wood, what would your machine look like?

3. If you had three wheels and could use them on a car, what would your car look like?

4. Now make a model of a three-wheeled object.

UP--UP--AND--AWAY

After studying about many of the things needed to make plants grow, have the children take a survey of how many adults think plants grow when they are talked to. Then put the results on the graph shown here.

YES | NO | DON'T KNOW

A PLANT IS WHAT IT EATS!

When working on a plant unit, don't forget to do experiments with color! After discussing the tubes that carry water and nutrients to all parts of the plant, ask the children to put a stalk of celery into a glass of red food coloring and water. Have each child write down on a piece of paper exactly what they think will happen. Collect the papers.

The next morning, group the children in pairs and have them examine the celery and complete the observation activity sheets on pages 116 and 117. After they are completed, discuss their findings in a group.

Name _____ Date _____

RED CELERY ??

Directions: Discuss the answers to the following questions with your partner. Write your answers to each question in the space provided.

1. Describe the leaves of the stalk of celery.

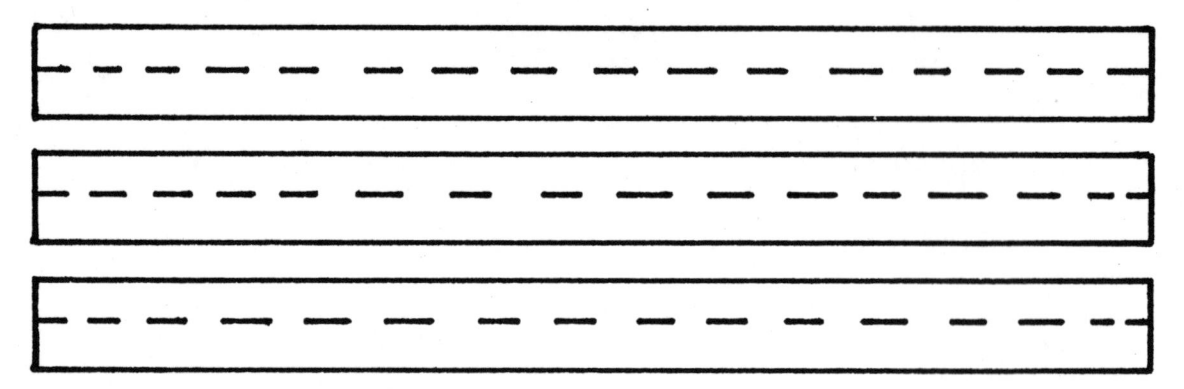

   _____

   _____

   _____

2. How did the red color get there?

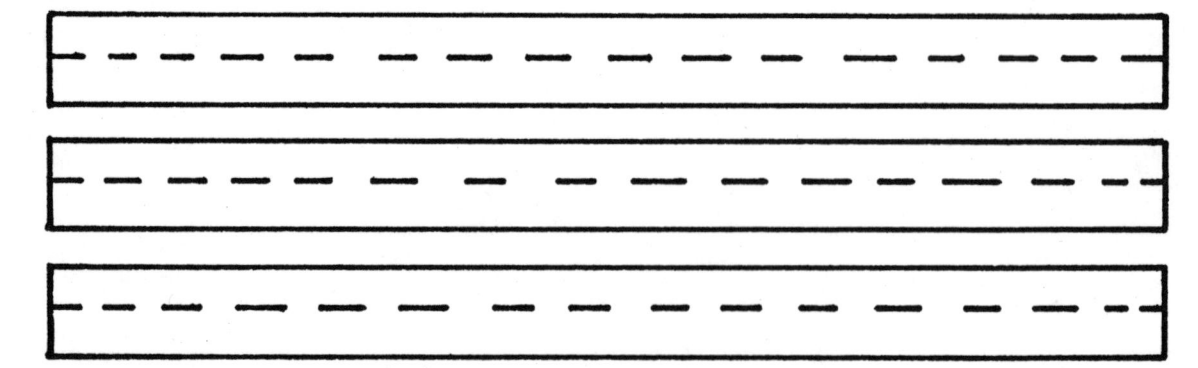

   _____

   _____

   _____

© 1985 by The Center for Applied Research in Education, Inc.

3. What other kinds of plants do you think could be used in this same experiment? List at least three.

4. Did you think that the celery would turn red? Why or why not?

Spiders, Spiders Everywhere!

A bulletin board can be an excellent teaching tool when working with bright students. Here's an idea that can be used over and over by just changing the content. Collect as many books, encyclopedias, and magazines on spiders as you can. Your students can search the library for the books you will need. Place them on a table near a bulletin board. Cut out the letters for the words "Interesting Facts About Spiders" and place them on the board. On a paper cutout of a spider, write the following directions and place it on the board:

118

Directions:

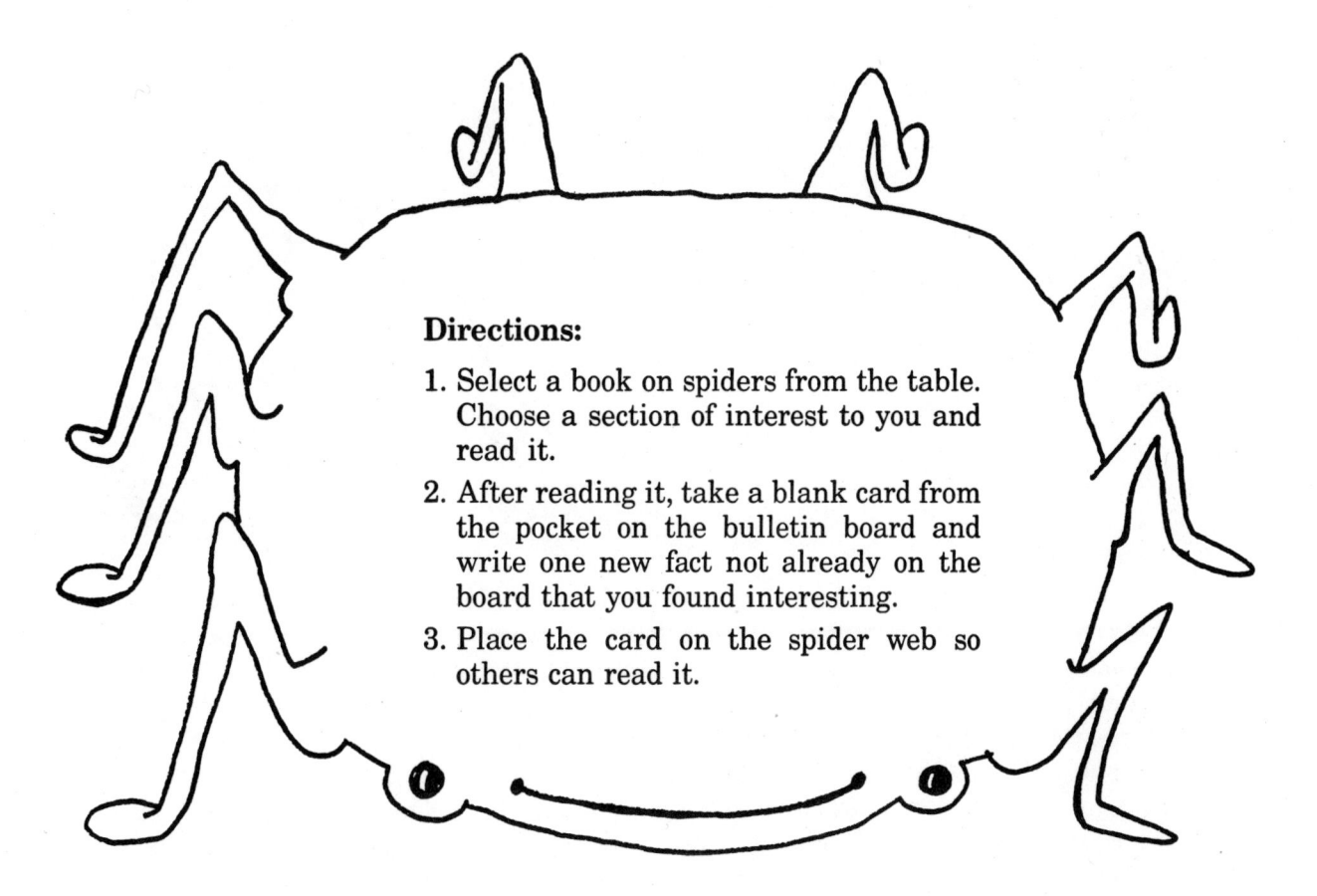

1. Select a book on spiders from the table. Choose a section of interest to you and read it.
2. After reading it, take a blank card from the pocket on the bulletin board and write one new fact not already on the board that you found interesting.
3. Place the card on the spider web so others can read it.

    The students will fill the board with facts and the entire class will learn a multitude of information. After several days, discuss the facts on the board. You should help the children to understand that much of the information that they hear about spiders is opinion or perhaps fiction. Discuss the difference between fact and opinion. When you are ready to change the board, take the fact cards down and staple them together. Have a child make a cover for the fact booklet and place it in your reading corner for future use. By the end of the year, you will have created your own library. You can also try facts about various sports, famous people, and periods in history. The opportunities are endless.

RAIN RAIN GO AWAY

Whether it's rainy, cloudy, or sunny, children always enjoy studying about the weather. There are always a few students in your room who, when working on a weather unit, are ready to do some graphing and predicting of the weather rather than studying what they should wear during certain kinds of weather. For these students, place a thermometer outside the building to be checked daily or, for more advanced students, several times a day at the same time each day. The weather information from the newspaper should also be brought in daily. This information will be used later and should be posted with your weather calendar. A calendar that includes the temperature and sky conditions should be maintained within the classroom by the students.

S	M	T	W	T	F	S
		1 ☁ 46°	2 ☁ 43°	3 ☀ 60°	4 ☂ 54°	5 ☀ 53°
6	7	8	9	10	11	12
13	14	15	16	17	18	19
20	21	22	23	24	25	26
27	28	29	30			

If possible, the children should be the ones to determine what symbols will be used on the calendar. (☁ ☂ ☀) If the children record the temperature several times during the day, they can then be taught how to derive an average. For example, suppose the temperatures are 54, 56, 59. If those numbers are added together (54 + 56 + 59), you would get 169. Now divide that into 3 equal parts because 3 numbers were used. The number 169 is close to 170 if rounded to the nearest 10. Now count by 10's to 170 and divide it into 3 equal parts. The children should be given time to try to figure it out. You may see some work samples like this:

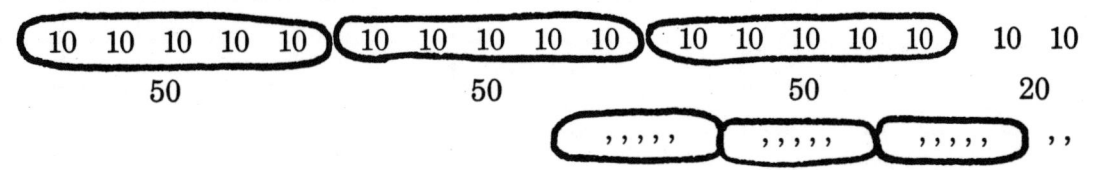

(10 10 10 10 10) (10 10 10 10 10) (10 10 10 10 10) 10 10
    50   50   50   20

(, , , , ,) (, , , , ,) (, , , , ,) , ,

Students will come up with an answer around 56° or 57°. What they have really been able to do is mentally divide. You should reinforce this and encourage mental calculations at a young age. Very bright youngsters think both abstractly and logically and can figure out a lot more than we think they can.

After recording on the calendar for two weeks, you can then help them graph their findings. For instance, how many sunny days, cloudy days, and rainy days were there during the two weeks that we recorded the weather? A pictograph is great for this.

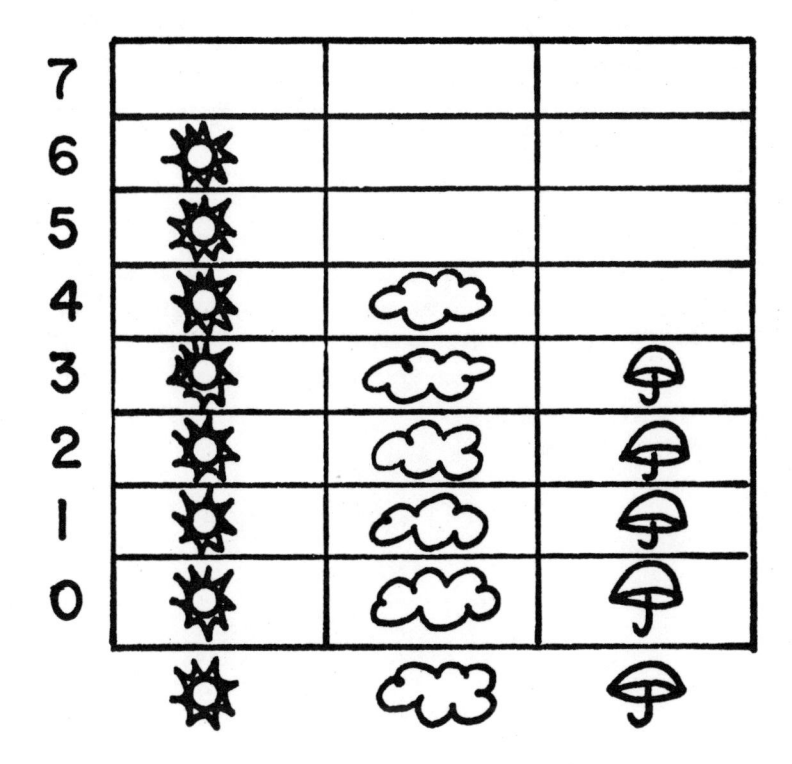

You can also have them record the temperature or average temperature on a graph.

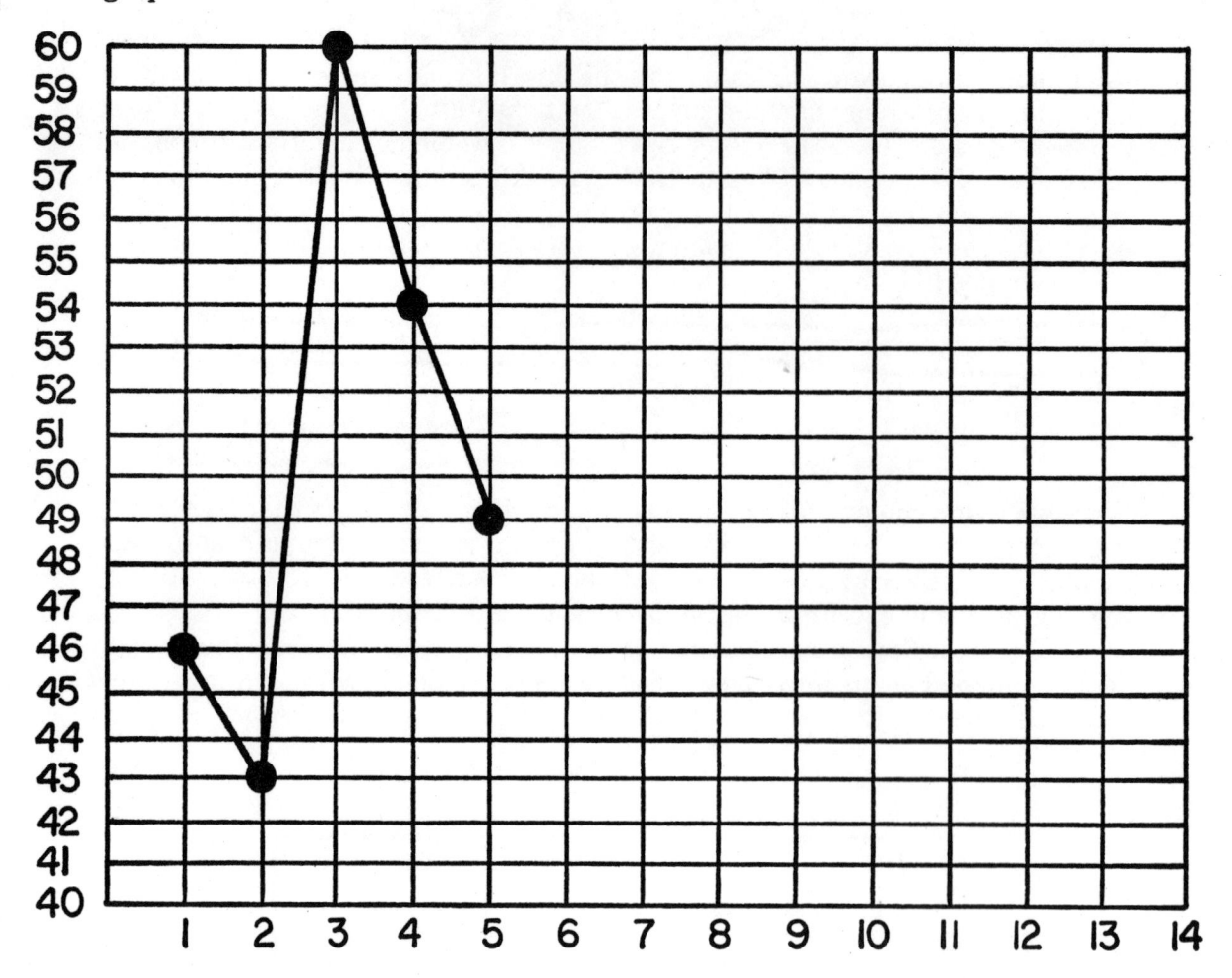

In the field of science, children should be encouraged to record, interpret, analyze, and predict from the information that they collect. They need to understand that the field of science is constantly changing. You may want to follow up with the "Sunny, Cloudy & Rainy Days" activity sheets on pages 123-125 as it gives the children the opportunity to analyze and predict the weather from their own findings.

Name _____ Date _____

SUNNY, CLOUDY & RAINY DAYS

Directions: Using your weather calendar and graphs that you collected, answer the following questions about the weather.

1. How many days did you record the weather on your calendar? _____

2. How many sunny days did we have? _____

   Cloudy days? _____ Rainy days? _____

3. What was the highest temperature that you recorded? _____

   Lowest? _____

4. How much difference was there between the highest and lowest recording? _____

5. During the first week's recording, what was the average temperature? _____

   For the second week? _____ For the two weeks? _____

6. Consider the newspaper weather predictions and the actual recorded temperature on your calendar. Do you think that weather forecasting is fairly accurate? Why or why not? _____

7. Why is it important for you to know the weather? Make a list of all the things you can think of.

1	6
2	7
3	8
4	9
5	10

8. If you had to forecast the weather for next week, what would your predictions of temperature and weather be? Complete the chart below.

S	M	T	W	T	F	S

Why do you think the weather and temperature will be this way?

_____

_____

_____

9. Now record the actual temperature and weather.

S	M	T	W	T	F	S

124

10. How accurate were your temperature recordings for each day? Make a chart.

	My Recordings	Actual Recordings	Difference Between Recordings	Reason for Error
S				
M				
T				
W				
T				
F				
S				

11. Do you think a weather forecaster's job is easy? _____

Why or why not?

125

Name _____ Date _____

OUR FRIENDLY SUN

Our sun is the most important star in our universe. Do you know why? Try to answer the following questions.

1. What good thing does the sun do for your mother?

    ———————————————————————————

2. What good thing does the sun do for your father?

    ———————————————————————————

3. What good thing does the sun do for you?

    ———————————————————————————

4. This is what it looks like when the sun doesn't shine.

5. This is how I feel when the sun doesn't shine.

6. What keeps the sun from being seen on some days?

7. If the earth were covered by very thick clouds, this is what it might look like.

8. If the thick clouds stayed for a long time, this is what would happen.

9. I love our friend, the sun, so this is what I like to see outdoors.

Hooting About Polluting

Studying about pollution? There is plenty of it everywhere. This is an excellent opportunity to have your brighter students help others understand the various forms of pollution.

Divide the children into pairs. Now have each pair decide if they would like to photograph the beautiful and unpolluted or the ugly and polluted. (You will need to make arrangements with your librarian or parents concerning cameras, film, and developing.) Have each pair of children discuss the sights in their immediate surroundings that would make the best photographs to depict polluted versus unpolluted.

Now arrange for a deadline for the children to present their project. You will have to give plenty of time for photographing, developing, and planning a presentation. The children should be encouraged to display their photographs and be ready to discuss them with the class.

If the students show a continued interest in finding out more about pollution, you may want them to complete the independent study in Section VII, "Independent Challengers."

FOR THE BIRDS

Any kind of accessory equipment that you can think of always brings a flood of enthusiasm for children, especially when it is something new that has not been used before. Explain to the children how binoculars make it easy for us to observe objects at a distance without being close enough to disturb them. Discuss what types of things you might observe with binoculars. Make a chart listing these things. Walk around your schoolyard looking at various things with the binoculars and discuss their function. Have the children describe the difference between looking at an object with the naked eye and looking at it through the binoculars. Discuss the proper use and care of the binoculars and its importance. Then, for those children who are real bird enthusiasts, set up the following activity for them to complete.

Gather as many books as you can about birds—their homes, migration patterns, etc. Place these books in an interest center in your room. (You may want to decorate your interest area with paper birds flying above the center area or posters of birds near the center area.) Have the children begin to identify various birds when you are on the playground, and record their findings on a class chart in your room. Then, using the books and materials, find out the following information about the birds—what their homes are made of, what areas of the country they live in, unusual habits they may have. Let the children add this information to the chart as it is found. Here is an example.

	Name of Bird	Number Sighted	Bird Homes	Location of Homes	Unusal Habits or Information
1.	Cardinal	3			Va. State Bird Male-Red (Pretty) Female-(Dark Red) Spotted Eggs
2.					
3.					
4.					

After several weeks of observation, have the child graph his or her findings as to the number of birds sighted in a picture graph like the one here.

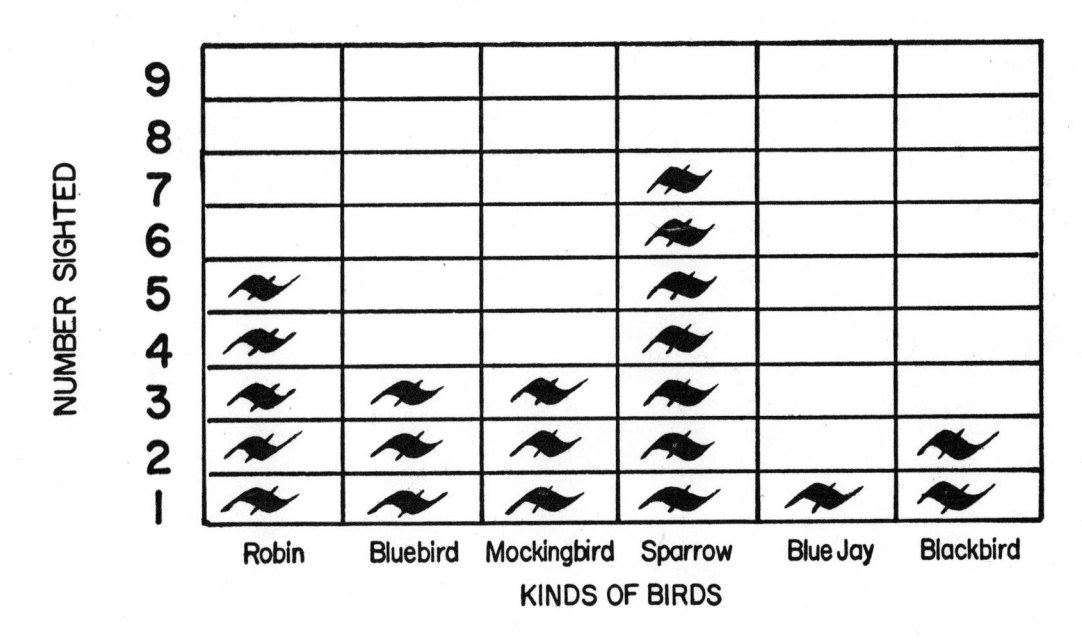

Help the children make generalizations about the questions below:

1. What are the most prominent kinds of birds found in our school area?
2. If you were to go somewhere else in our state, what kinds of birds would you see most often? Why?
3. Of the birds that were sighted, what bird did you think was most interesting to observe? Why?
4. From your readings, what kind of bird would you like to observe that we did not see?
5. If you were a bird, what kind would you be? Why? What things would you enjoy most about being a bird? Least?

As a follow-up you might talk about bird watching as a hobby and invite a bird-watching enthusiast to visit your classroom.

For those children who have truly become bird watchers and would like to venture out on their own, you might like to have them complete the independent study in Section VII, "Independent Challengers."

THE MICROSCOPE MYSTERY

Looking through the microscope is a new and exciting experience for young children. They see things that they didn't know existed because they were not visible to the naked eye. Allow the children to experiment with looking at different things under the microscope after explaining its proper use. They may want to look at a piece of hair, yarn, leaf, etc. You may also want to provide some prepared slides from your library or science lab. After you have allowed some time for the children to explore various items under the microscope, you can begin the following activity.

Have a small group of children fill a jar halfway with tap water. Take out a few drops of the water for the children to observe under the microscope. After they have observed the water droplets, have the children draw a picture of what they saw. Then record what they saw on a classroom chart that will be maintained throughout the activity. Your classroom chart might look like the one shown in the illustration.

Slide Observed	Date Observed	Description of Slide	Changes Observed
1. Tap water droplet			
2.			
3.			
4.			
5.			

Now add grass, roots, and leaves to your jar of water and let it sit in the sunlight or in a window with direct light. The following day, take a drop or two of water out of the jar and have the children observe it under the microscope. They should again draw a picture and record what they saw on the class chart. (Be sure to date their drawings so they can compare them at the end of this activity).

Continue this procedure each day until small moving animals appear under the microscope. When this happens, record it, draw a picture of what you see, and be ready to help the children figure out the answers to the following questions.

1. What do you think you saw?
2. Where did it come from?
3. How does it live in water?
4. What does it eat?
5. What will happen if the water dries up in the jar?

Have each child speculate about the possible answers to the questions. You may want to use the "Microscope Magic" activity sheets on pages 135 and 136.

After the students have had the opportunity to predict the "whys," supply some books that will help them verify or find out the correct answer to each question. Have them record the answers on the activity sheet.

Now have the children place their activity sheets and drawings in a booklet. Allow time for them to compare their drawings and to talk about the changes that occurred.

Discuss the activity thoroughly with the children, using your classroom chart. Discuss their calculated guesses and their findings about the small animals in the jar. Speculate about similar experiments that could be done at home or in the classroom.

Name _____ Date _____

MICROSCOPE MAGIC

☆

Directions: Write the answers to each of the following questions.

1. What do you think the moving object is? _____

_____

My Guess _____

☆

_____

My Findings _____

_____

2. Where did it come from?   ☆

☆

_____

My Guess _____

_____

My Findings _____

_____

_____

135

3. How does it live in water?

My Guess

My Findings

4. What does it eat?

My Guess

My Findings

5. What will happen if the water dries up in the jar?

My Guess

My Findings

ANTS, ANTS EVERYWHERE

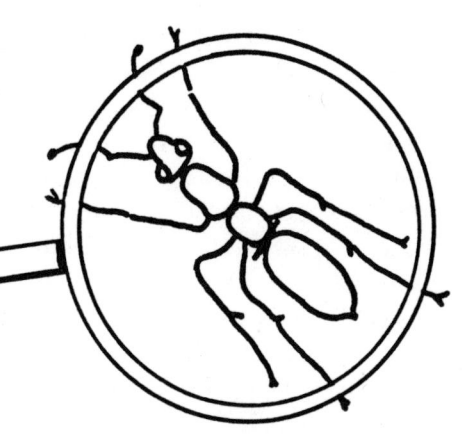

Using any kind of special tool brings about enthusiasm for learning in the classroom. What better way can there be to teach children about the changing field of science than through the use of a magnifying glass and an ant farm? Using these two simple tools provides an interesting way to observe, record, and draw conclusions about data: a systematic method necessary in the field of science.

First, place a number of small magnifying glasses in the classroom for the children to use. Allow plenty of time for them to experiment with them. After using them in the classroom, discuss the function of the magnifying glass with the children. Be sure to focus on the following kinds of questions:

1. What kinds of things did you look at with the magnifying glass?
2. How are things different when seen through the magnifying glass? How are things the same?
3. Why do you think a magnifying glass would be helpful in studying about small living things?
4. Why do you think a scientist would use a magnifying glass?

After the discussion, share a new type of magnifying glass with the children—a large magnifying glass you can find in your library or science lab. Compare the difference it makes when you use a small magnifying glass and a larger more powerful one. Talk about some of the other uses of magnifying glasses. List them on a chart and add to the list as your activity progresses.

Uses of Magnifiers

1. to help build a model (making miniature doll furniture)

2. enlarge print in books for those who read a lot

3.

4.

5.

Now it's time to introduce the ant farm. Have the children talk about and record on the "Our Ant Farm" activity sheets on pages 139 and 140 all of the information they can about the ants that can be seen with the naked eye. After a discussion, have the children predict what differences they think they will find when using a magnifying glass to observe the ants. Allow time for the children to record their predictions on their activity sheets. After recording the data, give plenty of time for the children to explore the ant farm with the magnifying glass. Talk about the differences in observation with the naked eye and with the magnifying glass. Assign various children a 10-minute period to observe and record on their activity sheets what they are seeing.

After time has been allowed for exploration, discuss their observations with the naked eye, their predictions, and their observations with a magnifying glass. Discuss the importance of recording data for a scientist, and the use of various tools.

Over the next couple of weeks, leave the magnifying glasses out and allow the children time for further exploration of the ant farm. You may find some of the children recording data on their own. If so, the activity has been a success!

Name _____ Date _____

OUR ANT FARM

Directions: Answer the questions below at three different times:
- First —After observing with your eyes
- Second —A guess of what you think you will see with a magnifying glass
- Third —What you see with a magnifying glass

1. What does an ant look like? Describe it in words.

Eyes: ┌──────────────────────────┐

Guess: ┌──────────────────────────┐

Make a careful one!

Magnifying Glass: ┌──────────────────────────┐

139

2. What are the ants in the ant farm doing?

Eyes: _____

_____

Guess: _____

_____

Magnifying Glass: _____

_____

3. Draw a picture of an ant.

What I see with my eyes.

What I see with a magnifying glass.

I WANT TO BE A VET

Children love animals and most of them have pets—goldfish, dogs, cats, turtles, or birds. Many of the children already know that a veterinarian (or a vet) is a doctor who takes care of animals, but may not realize that an animal doctor needs to be trained just as their own family doctor. In order for the children to understand the responsibilities of a veterinarian, place the following headings and questions on a sheet of large chart paper.

	Veterinarian	Family Doctor
1. How long does a person have to go to school to become a doctor?		
2. What kinds of patients does the doctor have?		
3. For what kinds of reasons do patients go to the doctor?		
4. What kinds of treatment, shots, medicine, etc., does each doctor give?		
5. What are some injuries that require a doctor's care?		

After completing the chart with the students, discuss the similarities between a veterinarian and a family physician, as well as their differences.

Then, plan to invite a veterinarian to your classroom, or take a classroom trip to a veterinary hospital. Allow time for the children to ask questions and find out answers to questions that have arisen during your classroom discussions. Following the visit of the vet, you may want to use the "Jane and Kiki" activity sheets on pages 142 and 143 to enhance student decision-making skills.

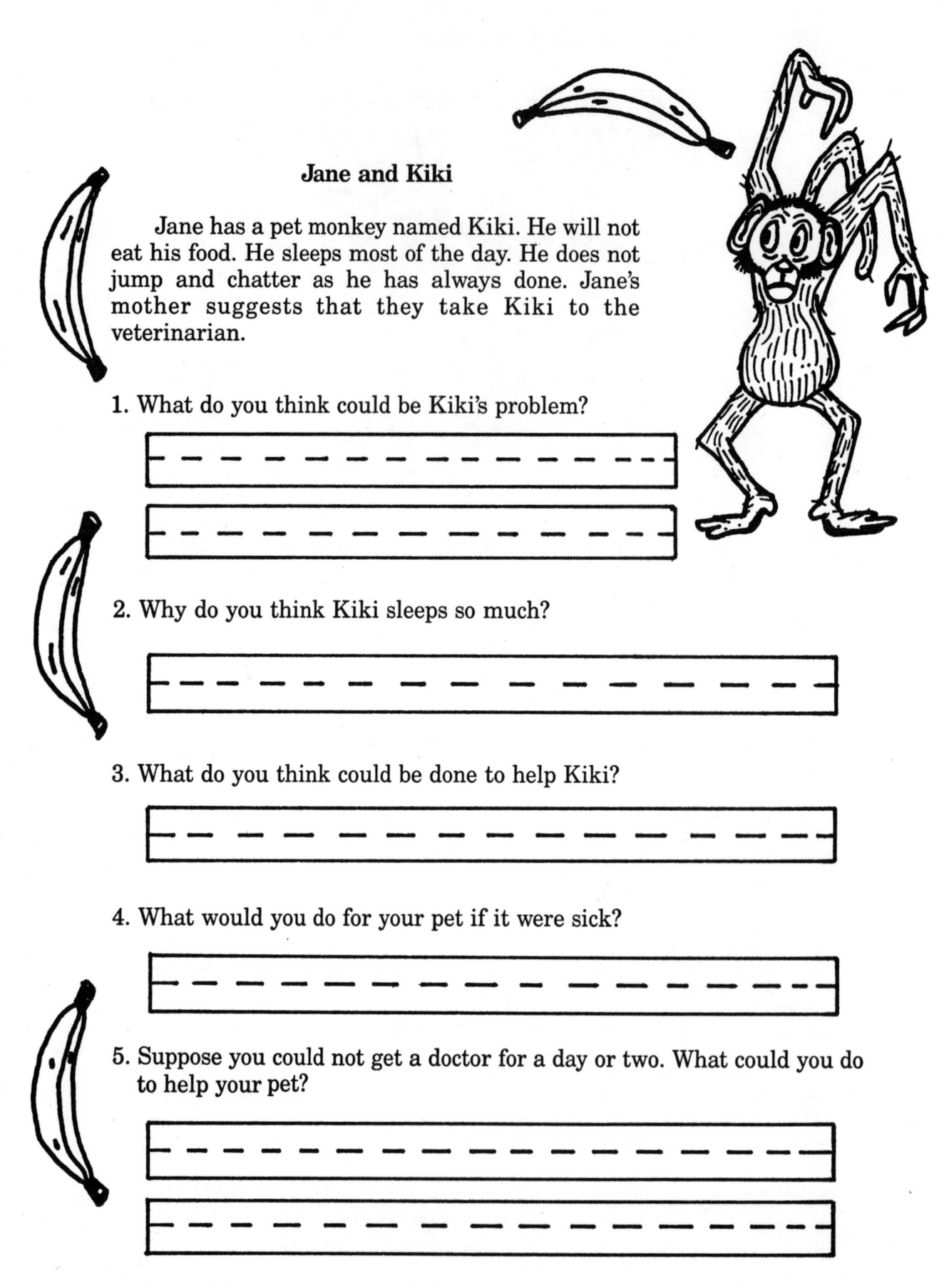

Jane and Kiki

Jane has a pet monkey named Kiki. He will not eat his food. He sleeps most of the day. He does not jump and chatter as he has always done. Jane's mother suggests that they take Kiki to the veterinarian.

1. What do you think could be Kiki's problem?

2. Why do you think Kiki sleeps so much?

3. What do you think could be done to help Kiki?

4. What would you do for your pet if it were sick?

5. Suppose you could not get a doctor for a day or two. What could you do to help your pet?

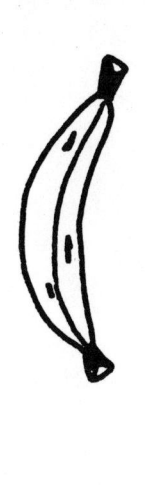

6. Why is it important to keep the pet warm and clean?

----

7. Make a picture of you helping your pet.

Section V
GLOW WITH
LIBRARY / STUDY SKILLS

Within this library/study skills section, you will find the development of many basic skills from alphabetical order and note-taking to locating information through the use of the card catalog. These library skills, although very basic, are generally not taught to the primary-age child. Therefore, it is necessary to give the young child the tools to unlock any new learning experiences in the library.

The major focus of this section is to teach these basic skills so that the primary gifted child can use the library effectively to find answers to his or her own questions and expand his or her own reading horizons. Within this section, the gifted child is given the opportunity to critique a well-known fairy tale and create one of his or her own, create his or her own card catalog, and even become a library detective in search of information about some modern-day monsters. Also included in this section is an activity that will provide the child with the experience of becoming a TV announcer or commentator. This will enable the child to get a taste of a career in communications.

Be A Bookworm...
Know your Library

Bright students are constantly asking questions and seeking answers. Just about the only way you can survive is to give them the keys to the library or media center. This allows them the freedom to seek their own answers and gives you another avenue to explore with gifted children. As early as kindergarten, bright students can be taught to use the card catalog. Once children can recognize the alphabet and put words in alphabetical order, you can begin to undertake simple tasks with them in the library. The following activities are designed to prepare the child to use the library. If the child has mastered any of the skills mentioned in the following activities, you can skip that particular activity and move on to the next one.

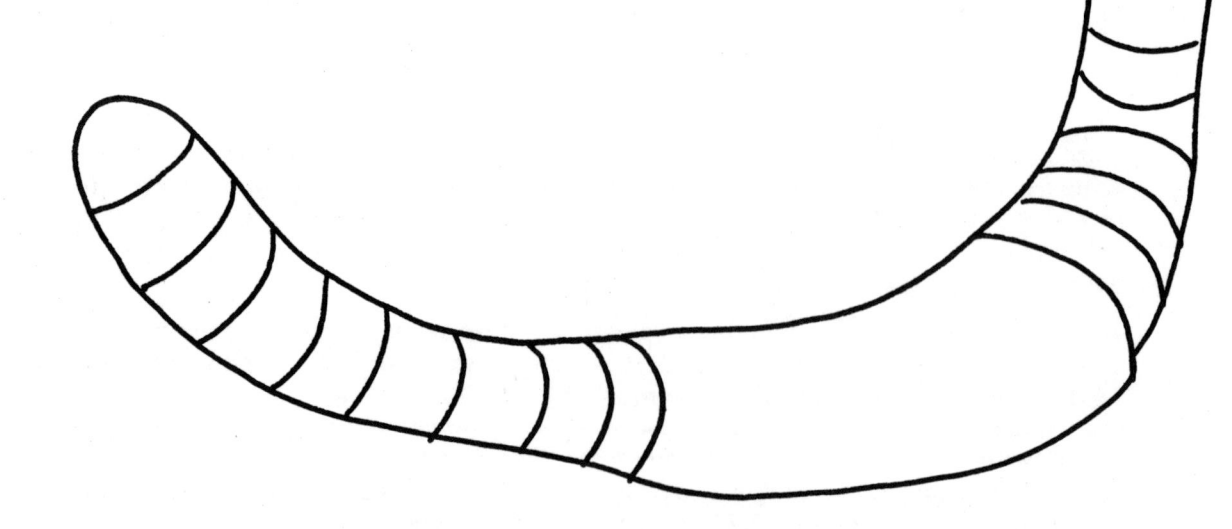

KNOWING YOUR ABCs

Using alphabet letter cards as flash cards, check to make sure that the young child can recognize the letters of the alphabet. If the child cannot, reteach this and then you will be able to use alphabetical order.

Write each of the children's names on a different card. Draw a box around the first letter in red. For example:

Bill   **Susie**

This will help the children to focus on the first letter in a word. Then have the children place the cards one by one directly under the letter that it matches on your alphabet chart. The children can then visually see why words beginning with A come first, B second, and so on. They can also understand why every group of words does not have to contain a word with every letter.

Repeat this activity several times using different word cards. After the children appear to feel comfortable, continue to use the word cards but place them in a row without the alphabet chart.

Now is the time to teach alphabetizing to the second letter. Using the same word cards, go back and put a blue oval around the second letter on each card. Example:

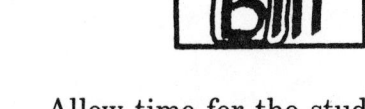

Bill   **Susie**

Allow time for the students to practice alphabetizing words to the second letter. Explain that it's a two-step process. Look at the first letter and put it in its proper place. Then, if a word has the same first letter, you must look at the second letter.

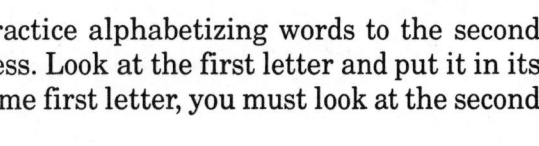

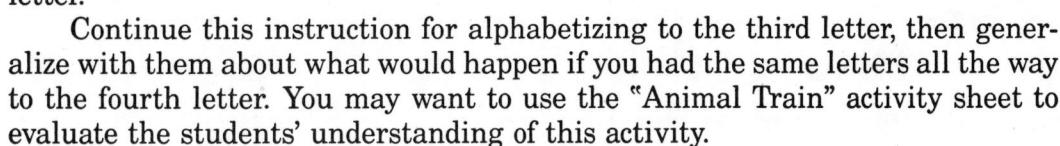

Continue this instruction for alphabetizing to the third letter, then generalize with them about what would happen if you had the same letters all the way to the fourth letter. You may want to use the "Animal Train" activity sheet to evaluate the students' understanding of this activity.

147

Name _____   Date _____

ANIMAL TRAIN

Directions: Cut out the words below. Glue them in ABC order. Three are given to help you get started.

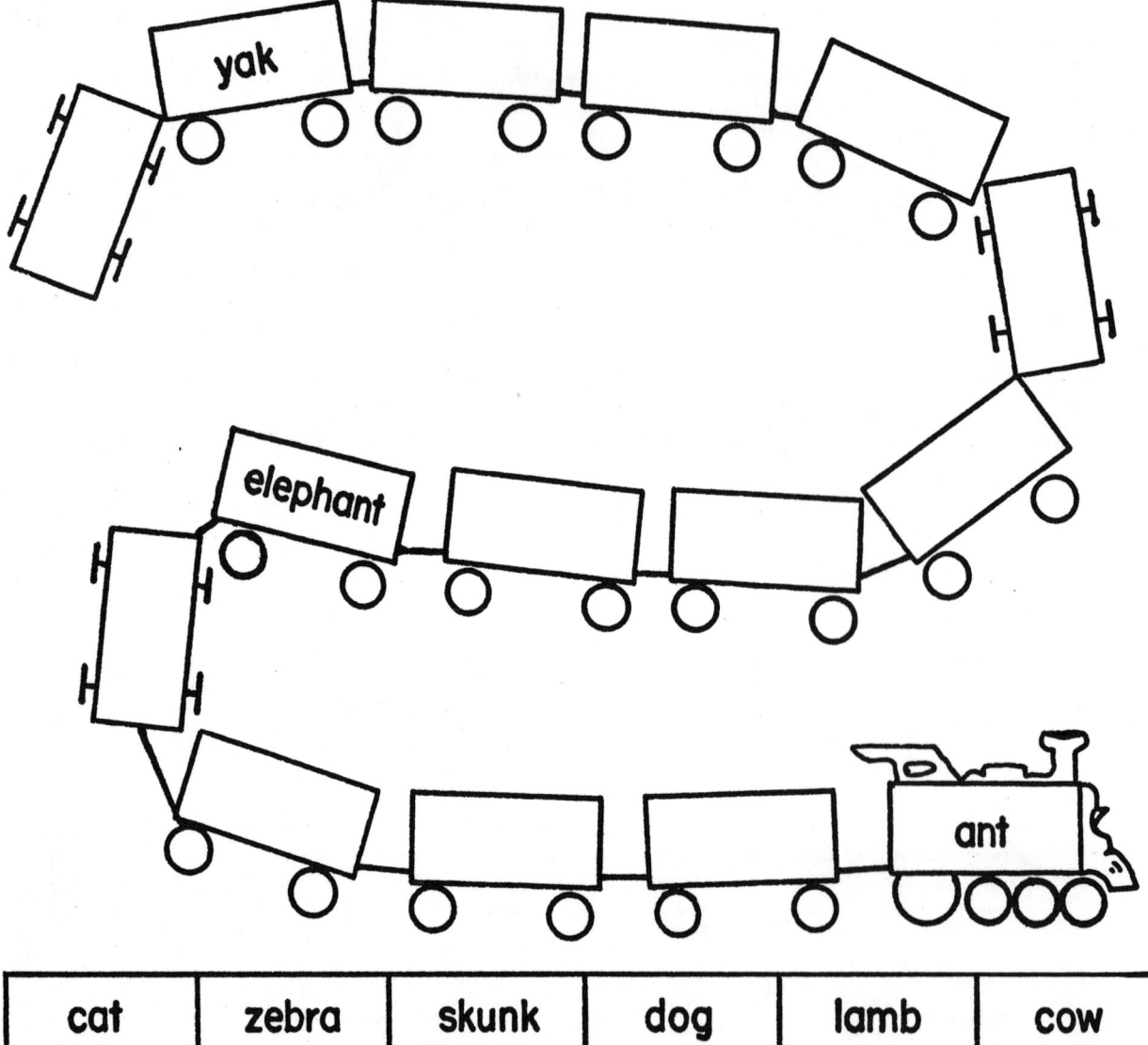

yak

elephant

ant

| cat | zebra | skunk | dog | lamb | cow |
| sheep | bird | giraffe | monkey | rabbit | deer |

Phone Book Madness

Have the students bring in the local telephone book, or you might want to acquire copies from your phone company as they can be used for many activities. This particular activity will give the children an opportunity to utilize their understanding of alphabetizing in another way. Place several names on flash cards and have the children find them in the phone book. Then, explain to the children that, like people, books have names and they are filed in the same way as the names in a telephone book, in alphabetical order. Also explain that this file is kept in a library and that there are so many books that they are kept in what is called a card catalog.

Take the children to the library to see the card catalog and allow time for a demonstration on how to find a book by its title. Then give the children an opportunity to practice what they have learned. You may want to use the "Look for It" activity sheet.

Name _____   Date _____

LOOK FOR IT !

A-B	C-D	E-F	G
H-I	J-K	L	M
N-O	P-Q-R	S	T
U-V	W-X	Y-Z	

1. Go to your card catalog. In which drawers would you find the following books?

   _____ *Cat in the Hat*

   _____ *Where the Wild Things Are*

   _____ *Biggest Bear*

   _____ *Katie the Kangaroo*

   _____ *Ping*

   _____ *Home for Bunny*

   _____ *The Egg Tree*

   _____ *They Were Strong and Good*

   _____ *Grandfather and I*

   _____ *Make Way for Ducklings*

2. Why would you find the card in the drawer you selected?

   _____

   _____

3. Suppose you did not know the title of a book you wanted. In what other way(s) might you find a book?

   _____

CUE CARDS

On another day, have the children tell you a subject they would like to read about. Make a list of these on a chart or the blackboard. Then ask the children how they think they could find a book about each of the subjects. List the ways that they suggest, encouraging any answer that may deal with the card catalog. Discuss the different ways and which ones would be the most thorough and the least time consuming. Go to the library and use the card catalog to find some of the subjects. Using a pad, have the children make a list of the books that sound interesting. This is an excellent time to point out:

- a title card
- a subject card
- synopsis of book on each card
- call number
- author's name (this may lead to discussion of an author card)

Talk about the importance of writing down the call number, author's name, and title of the book. Also discuss how to find the book easily in the library. You may want the students to complete the "Library Search" activity sheet found in Section VII, "Independent Challengers."

There is no better way for the children to acquire a full understanding of the card catalog than to make one of their own. For each book they read, have them make an author card, subject card, and title card.

Here is an example of an author card:

Seuss, Dr.
   CAT IN THE HAT

By _____

Have the children include a short synopsis of their book. This is an excellent way to teach children how to organize a project. Allow them time to work together to determine how they are going to organize themselves and their card catalog.

This will give you the opportunity to observe the leadership and organizational skills of individual children. You may need to structure the development of the card catalog depending upon the age of the students. Remember, first graders can do this activity if you use 5" × 8" index cards and require only one or two sentences about the book. As the card catalog grows, so will the children's enthusiasm. This is a great incentive for reading. The cards can always be counted and divided by three to determine how many books have been read by the students in your group.

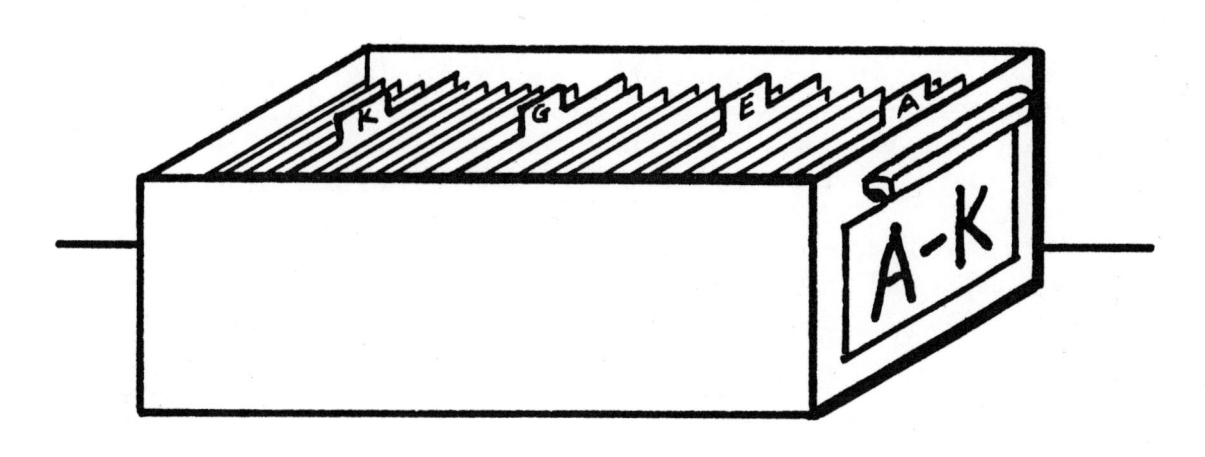

USE YOUR ENCYCLOPEDIA

When teaching the use of encyclopedias, you will want to tell your students a little about them. For example: a set of encyclopedias contains information on just about everything you would like to know, it is usually made up of many books, and each book is labeled with letters of the alphabet in order to help locate information.

Have the children choose one of these "modern monsters" and use the encyclopedia to find out more about it. Have them answer the questions on the appropriate activity sheet. (See pages 156-158.)

BIG FOOT

ABOMINABLE SNOWMAN

LOCH NESS MONSTER

After answering the questions, have the children write their answers in complete sentences on strips of paper. For example:

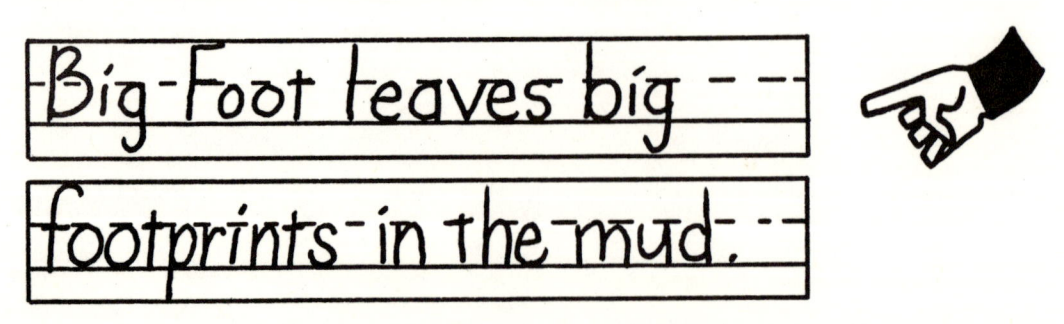

Big Foot leaves big footprints in the mud.

When all of the answers have been put on strips of paper, have the children arrange them to tell a simple story about their monster.

Now draw a large outline of the monster and cut it out. Details may be added for effect (bulging eyes, yarn hair, paper claws, etc.) When the monster is complete, have the children paste the strips of paper onto the body in correct story order. Be sure to display the monsters and share the stories with other groups.

LOCH NESS MONSTER

1. Where does this monster live?

2. What does it look like?

3. What has been done to try to prove that it exists?

4. What is its nickname?

5. Do you think it really exists? Why or why not?

ABOMINABLE SNOWMAN

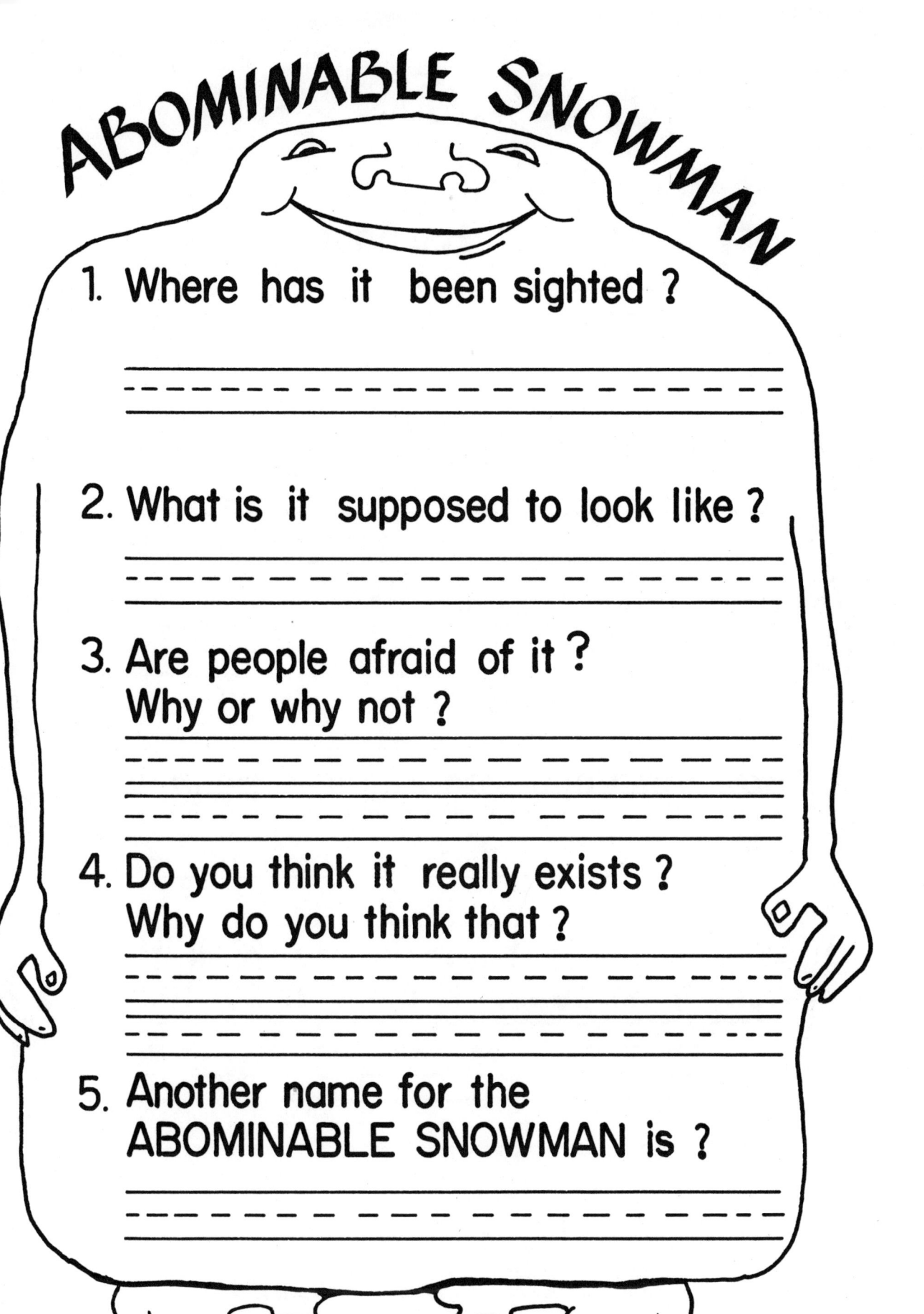

1. Where has it been sighted?
   _____
   _____

2. What is it supposed to look like?
   _____
   _____

3. Are people afraid of it?
   Why or why not?
   _____
   _____
   _____

4. Do you think it really exists?
   Why do you think that?
   _____
   _____
   _____

5. Another name for the ABOMINABLE SNOWMAN is?
   _____
   _____

BIG FOOT

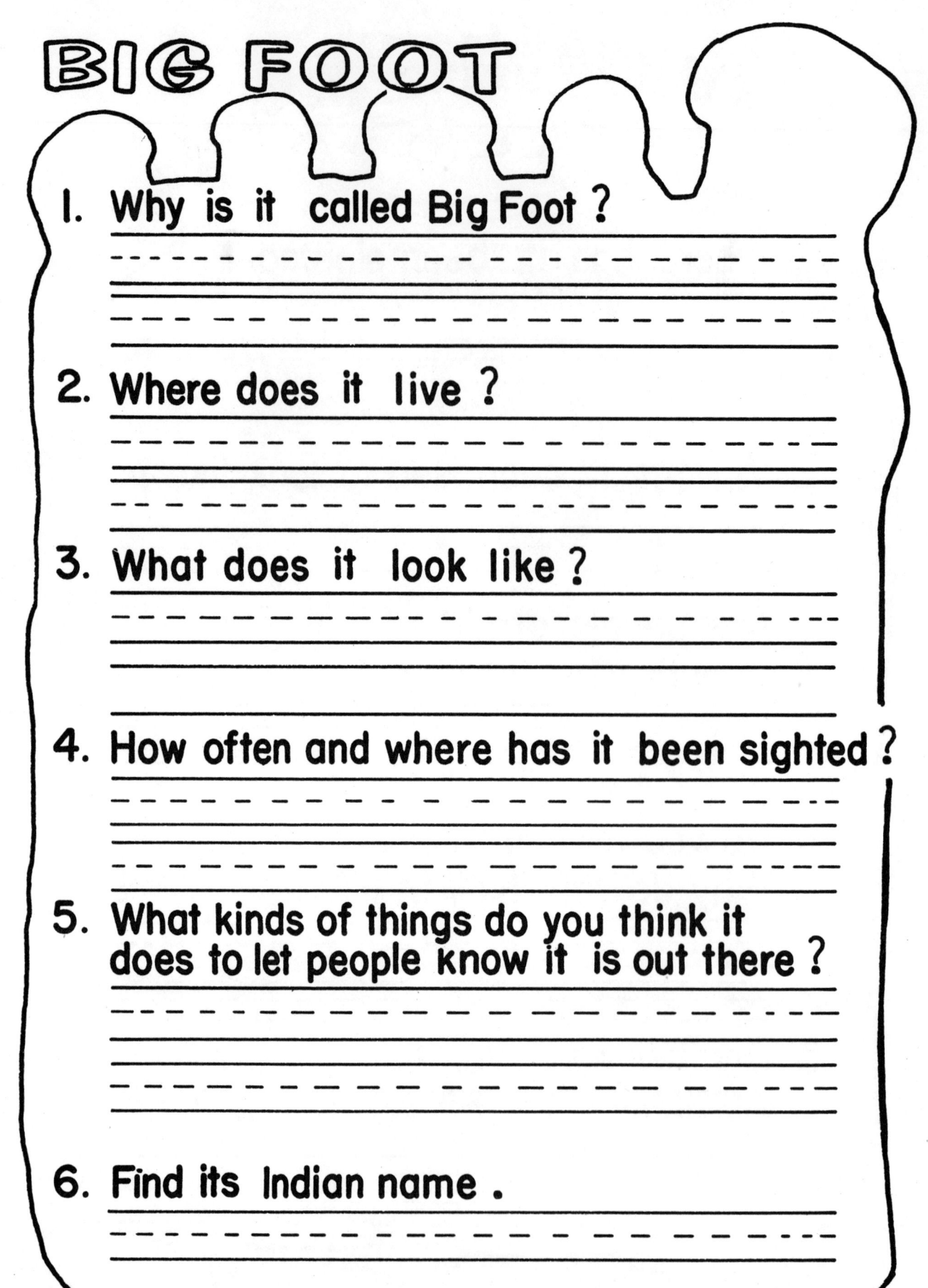

1. Why is it called Big Foot?

2. Where does it live?

3. What does it look like?

4. How often and where has it been sighted?

5. What kinds of things do you think it does to let people know it is out there?

6. Find its Indian name.

THE SHAPE OF THINGS

To open a unit on animals, or as a culminating activity, the bright children in your classroom may benefit from going to the library and reading as much as possible about an animal of their choice. This reading should preferably be nonfiction and should include a variety of sources—library books, encyclopedias, filmstrips, and charts.

As each book or graphic piece is read and observed, notes should be taken to aid the child in remembering important and interesting facts about the animal. This may take several days of research.

Using all notes and information, the child will then write his or her own fact book about the animal and make it into the shape of that animal. You will probably need to help the child make a pattern to use in cutting out the shape for the pages of the book. Here is an example.

Here are some things for the students to consider when making the books:

1. Make a simple pattern.
2. Have the teacher, aide, or parent put lines on the paper.
3. Decorate and laminate the cover for protection.
4. Use heavy metal rings to hold the book together.

After the books are completed, ask the librarian to set aside a special table to display your children's works.

It Happened Just So!

The library is an exciting and interesting place for young children to explore. You can begin this activity by allowing the children to utilize their card catalog skills. Send a few children to the library to find as many books as they can that were written by Rudyard Kipling. When they return with the books, put them on display somewhere in your room where they are accessible to the children.

You will then want to discuss with the children who Kipling was, and the purpose of his stories. If you have students who are capable of collecting this information and sharing it with the class, another visit to the library will be needed.

After the children have a brief understanding of the author, you will want to read some of the stories from *The Jungle Book* and *Just So Stories* to them. You may want to do this over a few days' time to allow discussion of the stories. Some of the stories you may want to read are: "Rikki-Tikki-Tavi," "The Elephant's Child," "Mowgli," and "How the Camel Got His Hump."

All of Kipling's stories are very interesting for the children, but this section will deal with the "How the...." stories—stories about how animals "got" the particular physical characteristic we associate with them, such as, the elephant's trunk, the camel's hump, and the leopard's spots.

After reading the stories, you may want the children to complete the "Wild Wild Animals" activity sheets on pages 161-163. This will allow them to create their own unique animals, each with an unusual physical feature.

Name _____ Date _____

WILD WILD ANIMALS

Directions: Read and complete each of the activities below.

A. Think of the five most unusual wild animals you can and write their names here.

1.	2.
3.	4.
5.	

B. What makes each animal unusual?

1.

161

2. [_____]

3. [_____]

4. [_____]

5. [_____]

C. Which animal do you want to find out more about?
[_____]

D. Where does it live?
[_____]

E. Why do you think its particular physical feature is helpful to it?
[_____]

F. How do you think it got that particular feature? (Make up your own answer.)
[_____]
[_____]
[_____]

G. Suppose it did not have that feature. What would it look like?

H. Give your animal's particular feature to two other animals and draw them here.

I. How would life be different for each animal with the new feature?

163

Name _____ Date _____

Little Red Riding Hood

Directions: Go to the library and find the story <u>Little Red Riding Hood</u> or listen to the story at a listening center. Now you are ready to complete the following activities.

1. Why do you think Little Red Riding Hood's grandmother made her a red cape?

2. Why do you think her mother allowed her to walk to Grandma's alone?

© 1985 by The Center for Applied Research in Education, Inc.

3. What would you have done if you had met a talking wolf in the woods?

4. What other animals could she have met in the woods other than a wolf? Think about how that might have changed the story.

5. Do you think Little Red Riding Hood really believed that the wolf was Grandma? Why or why not?

6. Do you like the ending of the story? How would you change it to make a funny ending?

7. Now, create your own version of the story on the story activity page that follows. You might want to draw your own picture of Little Red Riding Hood here.

Name _____ Date _____

Directions: Change the story <u>Little Red Riding Hood</u> in <u>one</u> or <u>more</u> of the following ways. Write your new story below and give it a new title.

1. Change the main character to a boy.
2. Change the animal and what happens with the animal.
3. Change the ending of the story.
4. Change any aspect of the story that you would like.

- -
(title)

- -

- -

- -

- -

© 1985 by The Center for Applied Research in Education, Inc.

BE A LIBRARY DETECTIVE

Many bright or gifted children are perfectionists in all that they do. It is very important that they be given encouragement and reinforcement for a job well done.

On page 169, you will find a certificate that can be used to provide reinforcement for library skills mastery. You may want to maintain a chart in your classroom that itemizes the library skills to be accomplished. A sticker or star can be used for marking mastery of individual skills. After a student has accomplished all of the skills and is a true "Library Detective" the certificate can be awarded for an outstanding effort and job.

LIBRARY DETECTIVE

THIS CERTIFIES THAT

_____

CAN USE THE LIBRARY EFFECTIVELY TO FIND BOOKS AND INFORMATION TO COMPLETE ASSIGNED CLASS PROJECTS.

_____ SIGNED

_____ DATE

© 1985 by The Center for Applied Research in Education, Inc.

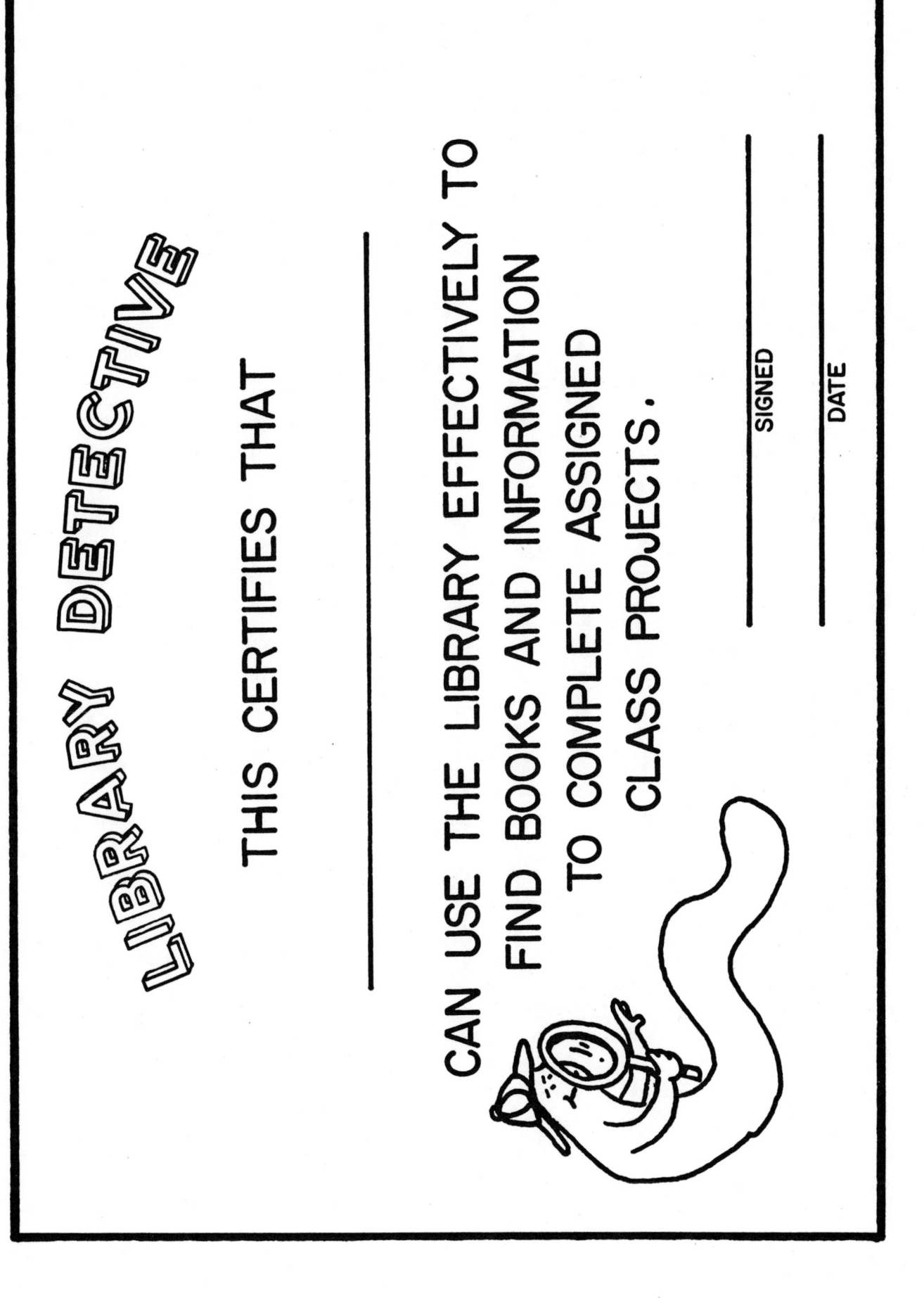

ANNOUNCING

EBS-TV

Very few children realize the hard work and practice it takes to be a good TV announcer or commentator.

Talk with the children about the occupation of TV announcer or commentator. On a chart, make a list of all the skills that they can think of that a TV announcer or commentator must possess. After discussing these skills, have the children watch a TV news show and/or a TV commentator at work. After watching the show, add any additional skills that they name to the list.

Now it is time for the children to have the opportunity to be a TV announcer or commentator. Have them select one of the following activities to complete, or encourage them to each present an idea of their own that they would like to try:

1. After a visit to a special location (firehouse, zoo, etc.), present a special commentary on the visit.
2. Give an eyewitness report of a sports event (a dodgeball game, a race between two classes, etc.) at the school.
3. Give a commentary on a school parade; describe the costumes, participants, etc.
4. Give an analysis of a movie recently seen.
5. Other

After the students have collected all of the information they will need and have planned their presentation, tape the presentations using the school's audio-visual equipment and play them back for the class to enjoy.

Discuss the problems they faced and the pros and cons of this profession. Add any additional skills they can think of to your chart.

Section VI
SPOTLIGHT ON CREATIVE ARTS

Developing creativity through the arts is a unique approach to stimulate the minds of our young gifted and talented children. The use of a stimulus with young children gives direction and sets parameters in which they can work. Once the children are ready to work on their own, the stimulus can easily be removed and the children can provide their own direction.

This section contains a wide variety of activities, from composing one's own music to experiencing oriental poetry and art. The children are given the opportunity to take an in-depth look at a potter's career as well as to do many hands-on projects including collage, creating their own comics page, and even developing their very own slide-tape show.

Also contained in this section are activities relating to well-known composers, and even the art of pantomime. As a culminating activity, the children are given the opportunity to select their own roles and play a vital part in planning, developing, and producing a stage play.

SHAPES GALORE

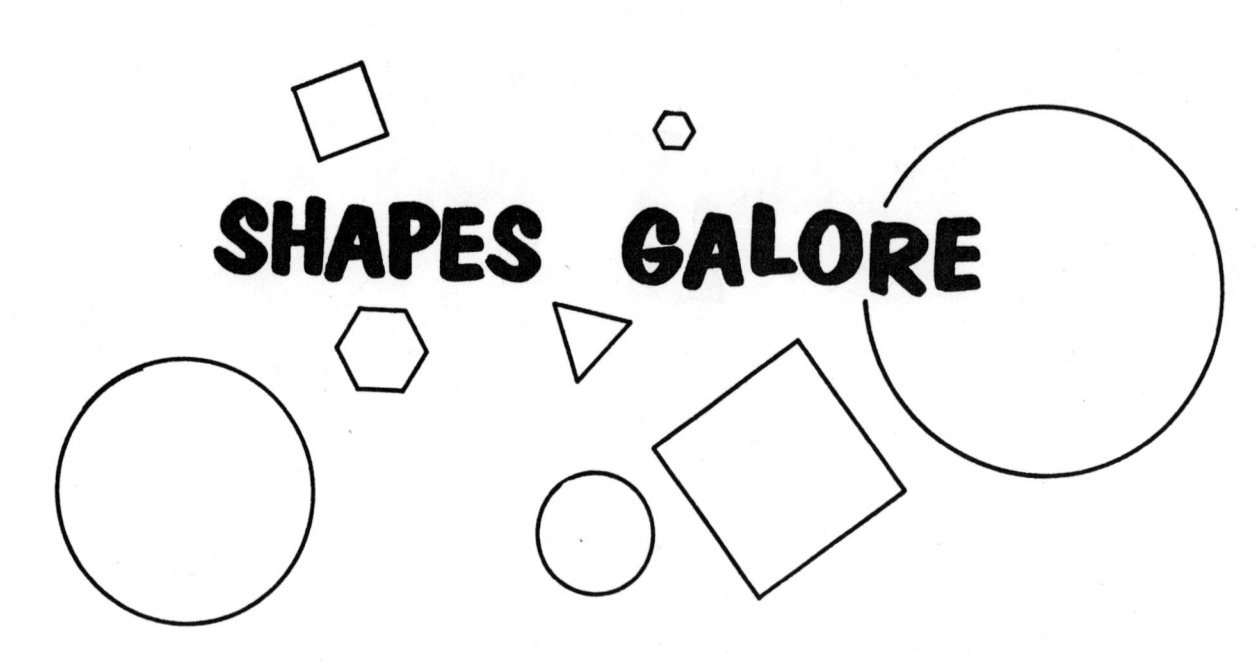

Encouraging young children to draw an unusual picture is sometimes difficult for the classroom teacher. Using shapes encourages creativity and helps the children to think about their drawing in a special way.

Cut out a number of different sized circles of one color. Give each child five circles. Then instruct the child to glue the circles anywhere he or she would like on a piece of 12" × 18" construction paper. Some of the circles may overlap, extend past the edge of the paper, or be entirely separate from one another.

After the circles are in place, demonstrate how to look at the circles and speculate about what they could be—a rabbit, a hippo, a lake, etc. After deciding on a composition, demonstrate how to incorporate the circles into the drawing, like the example here.

After the demonstration, have the children create their own pictures.

This activity can be repeated any number of times using various shapes or a combination of shapes. Have fun creating!

Heads-Up

One of your most difficult tasks is finding out about your students' interests, previous experiences, and their families. This requires so much time if done individually that it is sometimes neglected. However, this can easily be done by allowing time for the students to create a collage about themselves. This will give you the opportunity to find out about the children as individuals, and will help in planning individual assignments for all students, especially the very bright.

Each child will need a piece of posterboard for the collage base. The collage can be flat or three-dimensional, and hung. Each student should cut out a large silhouette of his or her head. On the silhouette the child should place objects, pictures, representations, etc., of things about him- or herself. Be sure to have students collect things (pictures, photos, awards, words from magazines, etc.) for several days before making their collage. You might encourage children to tell you all about themselves and include the answers to the following questions:

1. How old are you?   When is your birthday?
2. What is your favorite   color?   food?   sport?
   hobby?   person?   sports team?
   holiday?   lucky number?   school subject?
3. How many people are in your family? Who are they?
4. What especially interesting places have you visited?
5. What do you like to do when you have free time?

Before your students place their objects on the collage, be sure to talk about the techniques of developing a good collage—balance, textures, overlapping, etc. Perhaps you can have some collages on display in the classroom or hallway, such as reproductions of Schwitters, Braque, and Ernst.

JUNK ART

Making a gift for a family member or friend can be fun for small children, even if you instruct every move they make. Why not have your gifted and talented children use more of their thought processes in the creation of the gifts!

First, have a group discussion about some things that can be made using the contents of the junk box. Then write the suggestions on slips of paper and put them into a paper bag. Each child should then draw a slip of paper and try to create the object using the contents of the junk box. If there are other pieces of "junk" needed to complete the project, allow several days for these to be brought in, shared, and used.

- a hat
- a mobile
- a paperweight
- a birdhouse
- jewelry

POETIC SNOW PEOPLE

Creating snow people can bring out almost any child's imagination if given the appropriate shapes and accessories to stimulate his or her creativity.

To begin this activity, supply various sizes of ovals and circles (even a few odd shapes) and ask the children to select three to five shapes for their basic snow person. (These shapes should make a snow person about three feet high since it is easier for small children to decorate large objects.) Also, give the children access to a junk box filled with scraps of material, buttons, rick-rack, yarn, ribbon, silk or plastic flowers, etc.

When you have the materials, begin a discussion of ways to dress a snow person. This discussion will probably run the gamut from the traditional hat, scarf, and broom, to a sunsuit to keep the snow person cool when the sun shines.

After the discussion, allow each child to create his or her own person and share it with the class.

To extend this activity, you may use the poem provided, or make up one of your own.

Write the poem on sentence strips or chart paper and cut it apart to form strips. Give a random line to each child to affix to his or her snow person. The child then displays the snow person and sentence strip somewhere in the school building.

After all snow people have been displayed, allow each child in the group to go from snow person to snow person, writing down the lines of poetry. When the child has written all eight lines, he or she returns to the room and sequences the poem.

You can make this a self-checking activity by having your own snow person with the poem written in the correct order under the apron (or on the back).

175

Snow

The snow was light
As it came down.
The snow did sparkle
Like a beautiful crown.
The snow at night
Made no one frown,
The snow made a cover
Like a lovely white gown.

Carole Cook

Ask the children not to change the order of their poem even though it may be different from yours. As a group, share the sequencing of the poem. Some of the lines of this poem can easily be changed around. Discuss the reasons why the poem could be correct, sequenced in a number of different ways. Also, share some poems that could not be changed and discuss why. Allow time for the children to develop a poem with interchangeable lines about their own snow person.

PANTOMIME KIDS

To begin this activity, teach very young children how to play the game "Bum, Bum, Bum." The directions for the game are outlined here.

1. Divide the children into two teams. Place the teams facing each other in one long row.
2. Select one team to be "IT." That team selects an occupation to pantomime and keeps it a secret.
3. When the team members are ready, they march toward the opposing team saying, "Bum, Bum, Bum, here we come!"
4. The opposing team marches toward them saying, "Where are you from?"
5. The "IT" team says, "Pretty girl (or boy) station." (Girls say the word "girl"; Boys say the word "boy.")
6. The opposing team says, "What's your occupation?"
7. The "IT" team says, "Most any old thing."
8. The opposing team says, "Get to work."
9. The "IT" team then acts out the occupation it selected earlier.
10. The opposing team tries to guess what the occupation is and calls out the guesses. When the team has guessed the correct occupation, the "IT" team must run back to its side of the room without being tagged. Those tagged must be on the other team.
11. The opposing team is now "IT."

After playing the game, discuss the art of pantomime with the children. Talk about the different occupations that the children pantomimed during the game. Talk about what specific actions allowed the other team to figure out the occupation. Talk about animals the students could pantomime. Allow some children to demonstrate to the class. Make a list of action words on the chalkboard. Have a few children pick one of the action words to pantomime.

You might follow this discussion on pantomime with a film or even a visit by a mime artist. Each child should now be ready to put together his or her own mime show. Encourage the children to get help from parents, volunteers, or older children in the school. When the children are ready, have them perform their mime show for the class.

SLIDE SHOW

There are many interesting things to do with old slides! You and the children can bring in old slides to keep at school and use for a variety of activities.

One of the more interesting activities is to provide the children with viewers for looking at the slides. Have each child select some of the slides to aid in their creation of a slide-story presentation. Encourage fantastic connection-making.

The child will need to decide on the sequence of the slides and then create a story to be told orally as the slides are projected for the entire class. Notes or a completely written script should be given to the "editor" (teacher, aide, or parent volunteer). The editor will then make suggestions for grammar, expansion of ideas, or sequence. After revision, if necessary, the slide-story can be presented to the class.

As a follow-up, some of the children may want to choose a topic they are interested in, such as the family pet, and take several slides of the subject and create a story around it.

If there is a child who is really creative with a camera, ask him or her to write a short story about a topic of interest, and highlight the story with slides.

COMIC CARNIVAL ☆☆

Children always love reading the comics and are particularly attracted to comic strip characters. What better way to generate enthusiasm for learning than by setting up an activity where the children can read various comic strips and then create one of their own.

Have the children cut out their favorite comic strips and bring them to class. Post them somewhere in the room so the children can read them during their leisure time. After a few days, discuss each of the comic strips with the children. Talk about the different elements that comic strips usually have:

1. main character or characters
2. setting
3. plot or basic theme
4. humor or appeal to a particular age group

Together, as a group, think of a class mascot and develop a comic strip around it. Your comic strip may depict something special about your school, such as the school cafeteria. Draw your comic strip in colored chalk on the blackboard to show the students how it should be done. After the children have had an opportunity to develop a group comic strip, it's time for them to venture out on their own or in pairs. Encourage them to invent their own characters and to write about something of interest to them. When they are ready to commit their comic strip to paper, you may want to use a roll of freezer paper marked in sections so their drawings can be large enough to post in the room. This is particularly good for very young children. Adding machine tape also works very well for this project.

If you find you have a budding young cartoonist, you may want to submit the comic strip to one of the children's magazines or your local newspaper.

LET'S MAKE MUSIC

Making music on their very own instruments can bring a new excitement to young children.

Have the children fill six to eight tall baby food jars with varying levels of water. Now give each child a small wooden mallet or thick wooden pencil. Give each child the opportunity to strike the jars with the mallet and listen to the sounds that they make. Allow time for the children to experiment by striking the jars with various objects such as a plastic comb, a metal rod, or a ruler, and determine which sound they like the best.

Discuss with the children why some sounds are higher and others lower, and how the sounds relate to the amount of water in the jar. Have the children determine which jars to strike for higher sounds and which for lower sounds.

You may now want to pick out a simple tune, such as "Three Blind Mice" or "Row, Row, Row, Your Boat," just to show the children that songs they know can be played on their chimes. (You might want to record simple tunes on the xylophone and have the children listen to some of these.)

The children will certainly want to try to play songs on the chimes. They should be allowed time to practice and then given the opportunity to play their tune for the class.

After they are familiar with the chimes, students may want to create their own tune to share. When creating their own tune, students should write down the chime (jar showing water level) as they go. Then they can go back and play the tune again. You may want to use the "Chime Practice" and "My Chime Tune" activity sheets to allow your children to practice and create. You may prefer to use large chart paper for kindergarten and first grade children instead of the worksheets.

Name _____   Date _____

Chime Practice

1.
2.
3.
4.
5.
6.

182

Name _____ Date _____

MY CHIME TUNE

1. _____

2. _____

3. _____

4. _____

5. _____

6. _____

MUSIC MASTERS

Children from all areas enjoy music and especially have an appreciation for classical music. Even at a young age, children can tell the difference in style, mood, rhythm, and melody.

Choose two great composers who present music in different styles, such as Haydn and Tchaikovsky. Ask your students to listen to music by both composers and also find information from the library about their lives. (You might also play music from many great composers and let the children select two they would like to find out more about.)

After the information has been gathered, the children should complete the "Learning About the Masters" activity sheet.

Name _____ Date _____

LEARNING ABOUT THE MASTERS

Directions: Answer the following questions about the two composers you selected.

1. The names of my composers are:

   a. _____   b. _____

2. They were born in what country?

   a. _____   b. _____

3. They lived from __(year)__ to __(year)__ .

   a. _____   b. _____

4. I liked the music of _____ better because

   _____

   _____

185

5. I liked the music of _____ less because _____

_____

_____

6. My favorite musical piece from each composer is _____ and _____ because:

a. _____   b. _____

_____

_____

_____

7. Here are some interesting facts about each composer. They are interesting to me because:

a. _____   b. _____

_____   _____

_____   _____

_____   _____

8. Have you ever tried to compose music? ⬜ Try your hand at the school piano.

What was easy about it? ⬜

⬜

What was difficult? ⬜

⬜

⬜

Experimenting with Writing

Children are always interested in curlicues and fancy writing. Their interest is especially keen when they have learned how to write in cursive and want to experiment with various formations and letters. There is no better way to satisfy that curiosity than by teaching a new writing form—calligraphy.

Invite a guest to your classroom who has experience in the art of calligraphy. Allow time for the guest to demonstrate this art form and allow the children to try it.

After the demonstration, arrange to have an ample supply of slant-edge markers or calligraphy pens to be on hand in your classroom. You will also want to have an area in your room for a collection of books and charts showing basic calligraphy strokes. You may want to try using a colored chalk that has been slanted to demonstrate basic strokes for the children.

As the year progresses, allow the children to complete an increasing amount of work in calligraphy. Before you know it, you will find that you have some budding new artists in your classroom.

Encourage the children to utilize their newfound talents in many different ways within the school—printing programs for plays, making name tags, creating slogans and signs, and so on.

Haiku

Even very young children can love and understand poetry. Haiku poetry from Japan would be of particular interest.

Begin by reading several Haiku poems to the children. Then ask:

1. How are the poems alike?
2. How are they different?
3. What is the major theme or emphasis of the poem?
4. What pictures are created in your mind by the poem?

Now read the same poems again and point out their length, description of nature and season, and the picture it paints in the mind. Point out that a Haiku is three lines long, contains seventeen syllables, (five in the first line, seven in the second line, five in the third line), is about nature, and doesn't rhyme. You may want to "clap out" the syllables of one of the poems with the children. (Occasionally, because of translation, the poems may have fifteen, sixteen, or eighteen syllables.)

Give your children ample opportunity to read and listen to Haiku before they begin to write. Then divide the children in pairs and let them write Haiku to each other. Check to see that the four basic rules have been followed.

As the Japanese combine Haiku with beautiful artwork, you will want your children to complete the following activity.

On the top half of a piece of 18" × 30" unbleached muslin, have each child draw a picture of a scene to go with the Haiku he or she has written. Acrylic paint or permanent markers can be used. The child should then dip a large brush in a single thin watercolor solution and brush it across the muslin for a light-colored background effect. On the bottom of the muslin, the child should carefully write the Haiku with India ink or a fine felt-tipped marker. The material should be stretched and secured so the writing can be done easily.

When dry, the material should be folded and stitched at the top to form a casing for a dowel. The sides and bottom should be hemmed. Slip in a dowel at the top and the child has a beautiful Japanese wall hanging.

QUIET ON THE SET!

In this project you may want to combine your talented children with those of other teachers and/or grades.

After the children have written stories, acted in classroom activities, painted and made pictures, and showed others how to do various tasks, give them the experience of doing their own play with you as "advisor," only to keep things moving along when necessary.

You must first have your group decide who has a particular interest in each of the following things and sign up for one or two:

1. writers
2. actors
3. sets
4. costumes
5. directors
6. producers

You may need to explain the job of each to the group, so each person knows what his or her particular contribution is to be.

In considering the subject for the play, you may want it to follow a certain science or social studies unit you are studying. It may be the students' own creation of a familiar fairy tale, such as "Jack and the Beanstalk," or a particular interest the children may want to write about.

To begin production, the first thing you need is a play. Gather your children who signed up to write and get them started on the play by helping them outline exactly what they want to do. Then, when they have a good idea of how to go about writing speaking parts, let them try to do it.

While one group is writing the play, discuss what kinds of sets you will need with the set directors. Using the outline of the play will give them a good idea of what is needed. Offer suggestions to vary the usual paper mural background.

Give the producers the job of finding ways to acquire materials for the play. Since producers usually back plays financially, this should be a good substitute.

When the play is written and "edited," you will meet with your directors and actors. The actors will begin by reading their parts and "walking" through the scenes as the writers intend and the directors direct.

While this is taking place, you should put your group of costume designers into action. They will decide on the kinds of costumes needed and on how to go about getting them. They should also meet with the actors and the directors to discuss what type of costumes they think are needed and go back to the producers with any problems they may have in obtaining the costumes.

After all the sets are made, all the lines are learned, and the play is completely ready, have a dress rehearsal for other students to get out any "bugs." Ask the student audience to offer comments and suggestions for improvements. Then, invite the parents, administrators, and other classes to see the big production! Don't forget to have some of the students who are particularly good at handwriting or calligraphy make the program to be distributed. "Break a leg!"

MAKING POTTERY

Children love to work with clay, but few of them get the opportunity to really study about its origins, use, or the people who have made pottery their career.

Begin this activity by collecting and displaying various pieces of pottery for the children to examine. Be sure to display both unglazed and glazed pieces, painted pieces, and useful pieces.

After the children have had an opportunity to examine the pieces, lead a discussion about pottery. The first point that should be covered is what a person who makes pottery is called. The children should learn the definition of a potter.

> **Potter:** a person who makes objects from clay.

During the discussion, the children should be introduced to such terms as design, shape, and texture. The children should discuss the various tools used by a potter. They should also understand the history behind pottery including the following points:

- How ancient people made and utilized pottery
- The introduction of design to beautify pottery and how the designs are made
- Uses of pottery by modern people—bird feeders, tree ornaments, beads, jewelry, etc.

Encourage the children to find out some of this information on their own or invite a potter to visit the classroom and give a demonstration.

After the children have learned all about pottery, give them the opportunity to become potters themselves. Take the children to see a potter using a wheel to form vases. This *is* like magic. Let them try their hands at the wheel, too! After creating a number of clay objects, they will understand the difficulty of the trade and the importance of practicing with the clay.

Now provide each child with copies of the "All About Pottery" activity sheet.

Name _____ Date _____

ALL ABOUT POTTERY

Directions: Answer the following questions or complete the activity.

1. Why do you think people first started using pottery?

- -

- -

- -

2. What were some of the early uses of pottery?

- -

- -

3. How do you think early people decided which soil was clay?

```
_____
_____
```

4. When working with clay, why is it important to keep it damp?

```
_____
_____
```

5. What would happen to clay if it dried out?

```
_____
_____
```

6. If you could invent a new product made from clay, what would it be?

```
_____
```

7. Draw a picture of your new clay product.

8. If you were a potter, how would you display and sell your product?

How much would you charge for it?

9. Make an advertisement for your clay product below.

Section VII
BRIGHTEN YOUR DAY WITH

INDEPENDENT CHALLENGERS

The "Independent Challengers" section of this book is designed to provide opportunities for the primary gifted child to integrate skills learned from other sections of the book and to utilize these skills to complete activities with little or no direction from the classroom teacher. (It may be difficult for a child who has not used activities from other sections of the book to complete these activities independently.)

Many of the activities have been designed for a specific content area, but the general format of the activity could be easily changed to meet any child's needs. However, there are several activities included in this section that allow the child to select the content that he or she would like to examine. The use of outside resources as well as the library have been encouraged and the child will have the opportunity to integrate these resources into his or her learning experience.

The activities included in this section allow the child to observe and record as well as create. The child is given the opportunity to examine a career of interest and even predict how careers will change in the future.

A TREASURE HUNT

Hunting for treasure can be an exciting way to teach children how to follow directions and utilize their mapping skills. Place the following clues in the location designated.

Clue 1 – Give this clue to the child.

Go to the place where food is prepared and look under the salt shaker on the counter.

Clue 2 – This clue should be placed under the salt shaker.

Go to the place where you check out books and look in an encyclopedia about dogs.

Clue 3 – This clue should be placed in an encyclopedia about dogs in the library.

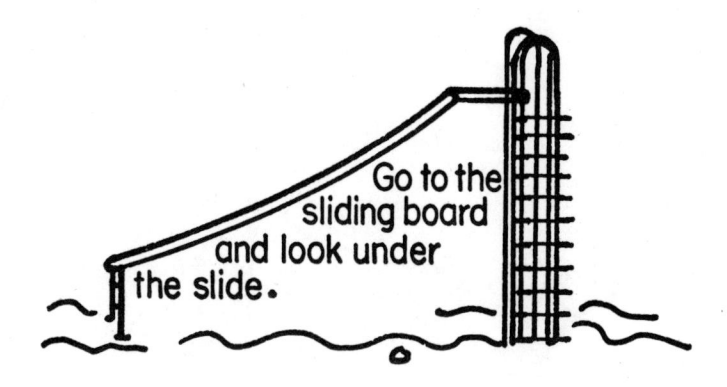

Go to the sliding board and look under the slide.

Clue 4 – This clue should be placed under the sliding board.

Go to the place where you sit and do your work and look inside to find the treasure.

Place a small treasure inside each child's desk. After the children have located their treasures, have the children draw a map of their route.

A treasure hunt is an excellent way to teach many skills, from research to analogies. Try developing another treasure hunt for your students.

Name _____ Date _____

A FLYING TEAPOT ??

Directions: Complete the following steps to help you develop an unusual story.

1. Pick a *number* from 1-10. Write your number here._____

  1. puppy 6. marshmallow
  2. snail   7. owl
  3. teapot 8. carpet
  4. rattlesnake 9. basket
  5. frog   10. train

2. Pick a *number* from 11-20. Write your number here._____

  11. whistled 16. melted
  12. sang 17. changed
  13. flew 18. bowled
  14. cried 19. played
  15. ate   20. grew

3. Now take the words that represent each of the numbers you selected and put them together to form the title of a story.
  Example: Numbers 2 and 13
       The Snail That Flew

© 1985 by The Center for Applied Research in Education, Inc.

4. Now, using another sheet of paper, write a story about the title you selected.

5. When your story is complete, draw a picture of the numbered item that you selected and paste your story onto your picture like the one shown here.

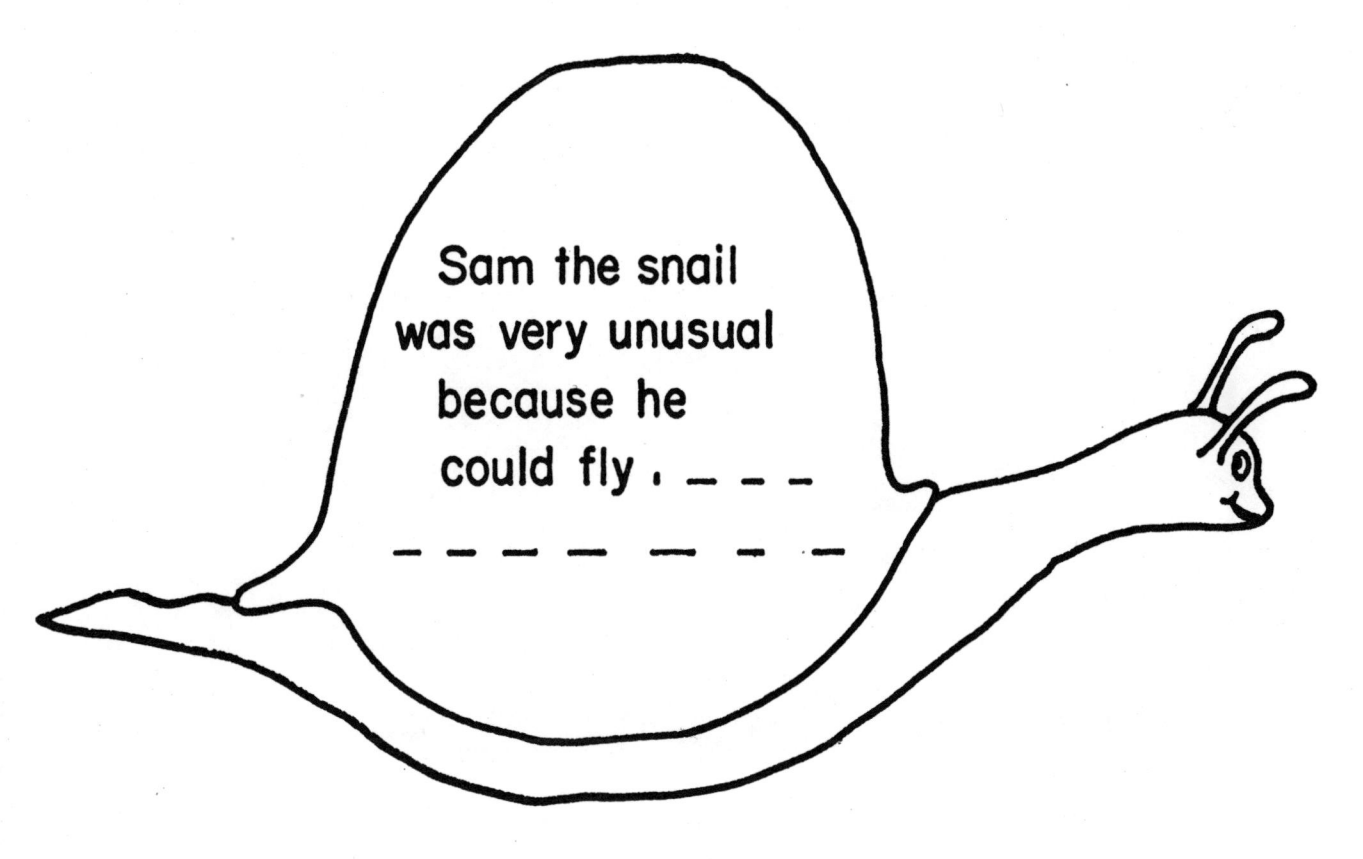

Sam the snail was very unusual because he could fly. _ _ _
_ _ _ _ _ _ _

Name _____ Date _____

TO POLLUTE OR NOT TO POLLUTE?
THAT IS THE QUESTION

Directions: Complete each of the questions or activities below.

1. Make a list of all the things you see that indicate that the above area is not polluted. List at least ten things.

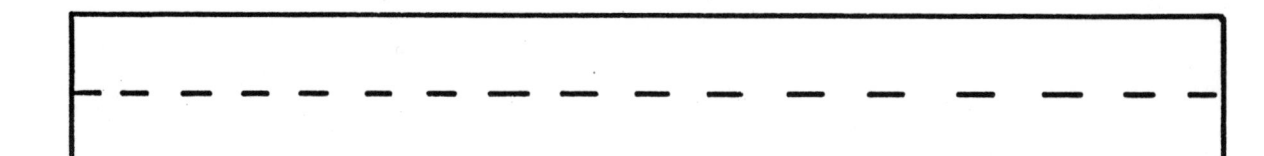

202

2. Now, if you were to place a car on the road with a family in it going for a day at the lake, make a list of all the things that could happen to make this a picture of pollution. List at least ten things.

3. Make a list of as many people or things that you can think of that are responsible for pollution. List at least ten things.

4. Think of some ways that you could help prevent pollution. Make a list below.

---

5. Share your list of ways to prevent pollution with a small group of friends. Encourage your friends to help you select one way that all of you can work together to prevent pollution. Write your choice below.

---

6. Now, with your group of friends plan a presentation to get your class to help you prevent pollution. Ask your teacher for help with the planning.

My Country 'Tis of Thee

Are your children working on patriotism? You may want to try some of the following independent activities for small groups of children in your classroom.

Activity 1. Give each child in the group a piece of chart paper. On the paper, have the children list as many things as they can think of that would be a patriotic thing to say. After listing them, have the students select one of their favorite sayings to make a patriotic banner. Here are examples.

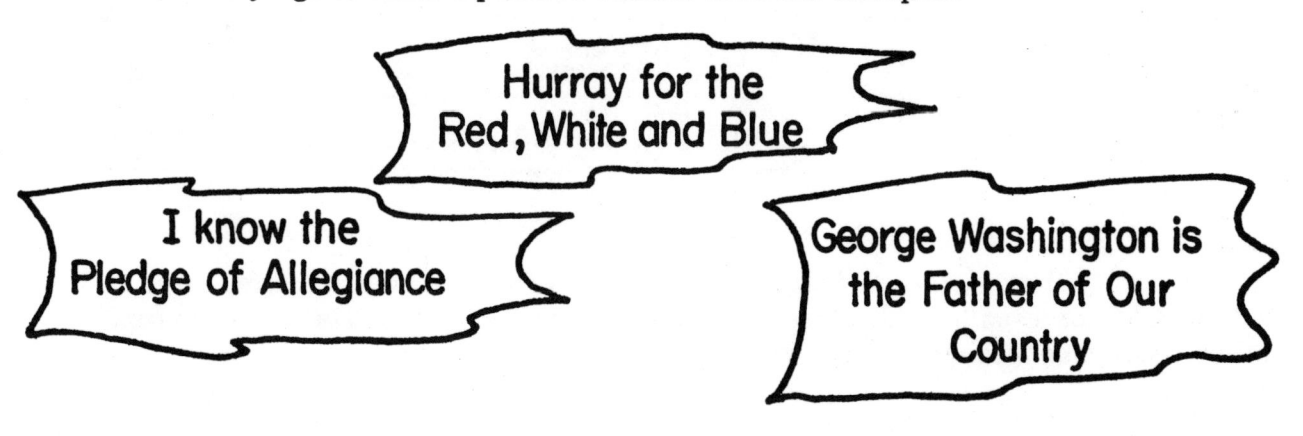

> Hurray for the Red, White and Blue

> I know the Pledge of Allegiance

> George Washington is the Father of Our Country

Activity 2. Give each child a list of people, places, and things. Have them place each item in a category. For example:

People	*Places*	*Things*
Abraham Lincoln	Philadelphia, PA	Liberty Bell
George Washington	Washington, DC	Declaration of Independence

See if the children can come up with a category that you didn't think of.

Activity 3. Have the children list as many things as they can think of that tell what an American is. Allow time for each child to share his or her list. Make a group list indicating the number of times the same answers were repeated. Then, from your list, make a graph of the most frequent answers. Here is an example.

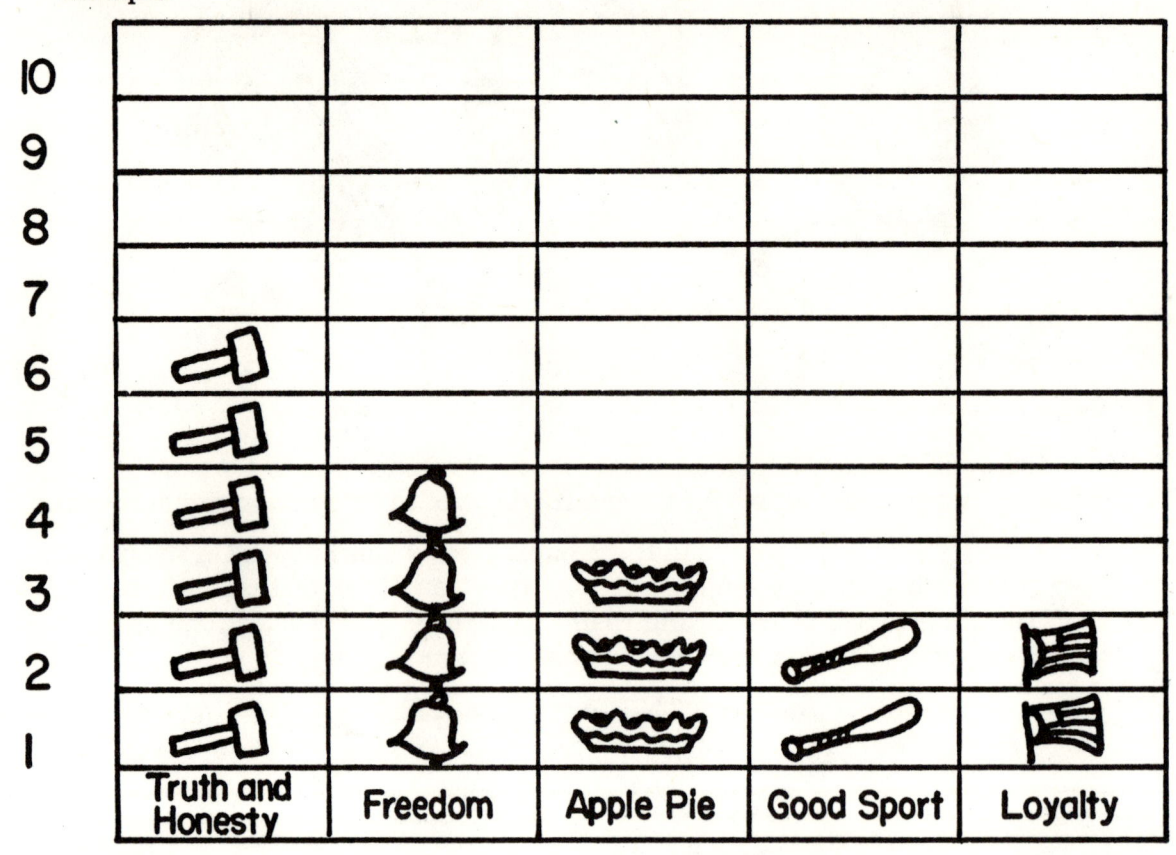

	Truth and Honesty	Freedom	Apple Pie	Good Sport	Loyalty
10					
9					
8					
7					
6	✓				
5	✓				
4	✓	✓			
3	✓	✓	✓		
2	✓	✓	✓	✓	✓
1	✓	✓	✓	✓	✓

Activity 4. Have the children make a list of all the patriotic songs they can think of. Then have them learn one new song to teach to the class or write one new song to an old familiar tune that they can share.

Name _____ Date _____

Experimenting

1. Name of experiment:

_____
- -
_____

2. Materials I am going to use:

_____
- -
_____

3. What I am going to do:

_____
- -
_____

4. What happened:

_____
- -
_____
- -
_____

5. Why I think it happened:

_____
- -
_____
- -
_____

© 1985 by The Center for Applied Research in Education, Inc.

6. Complete the following drawings.

Before	After

208

Name _____ Date _____

BIRD WATCHERS

Directions: Answer the questions or complete the activities below.

1. In your backyard, neighborhood, or nearby park, observe birds with a pair of binoculars. What kinds of birds did you see? (Hint: You may need a bird book to help you identify the ones you see.) Make a list of the kinds of birds you observed.

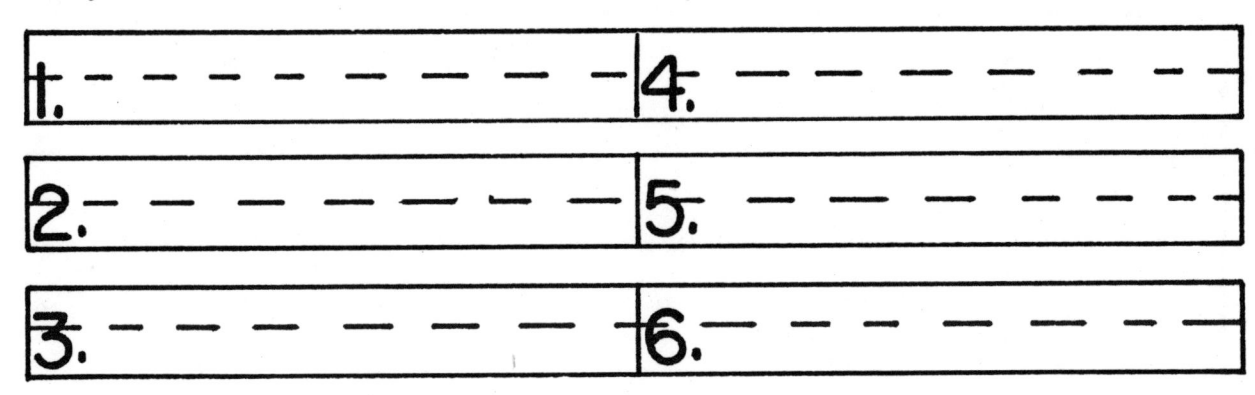

   1. _____   4. _____

   2. _____   5. _____

   3. _____   6. _____

2. Pick one of the birds to watch. Observe it carefully. Record what it was doing while you watched.

   _____

   _____

   _____

3. Draw a picture of the bird you selected.

4. Go to the library and read some books or find out some information about the bird you selected. Jot down some notes here to help you remember.

5. Now see if you can find an *empty* bird's nest in your observation area. Examine it carefully. What is it made of?

6. Now decide on a way to share the information you have collected with your classmates. Ask your teacher for help. Plan a presentation about the bird you have studied and present it to your class.

Name _____   Date _____

Library Search

Go to your school library and find the answers to each of these questions.

1. Write at least five things you would like to learn more about.

   a. _____
   b. _____
   c. _____
   d. _____
   e. _____

2. Think about these five things. Pick one of these things to find more about. Write your choice here.
   _____

3. Now, write what you will look under in the card catalog.
   _____

4. What kind of card will you find when you look under your choice? Circle the correct one.

   Author Card   Subject Card   Title Card

5. Fill in this card. Make it look like one you might find in the card catalog you circled in question 4.

6. What are some other places you might look to find out about your choice?

_____

7. Where do you think you could find the most helpful information?

_____

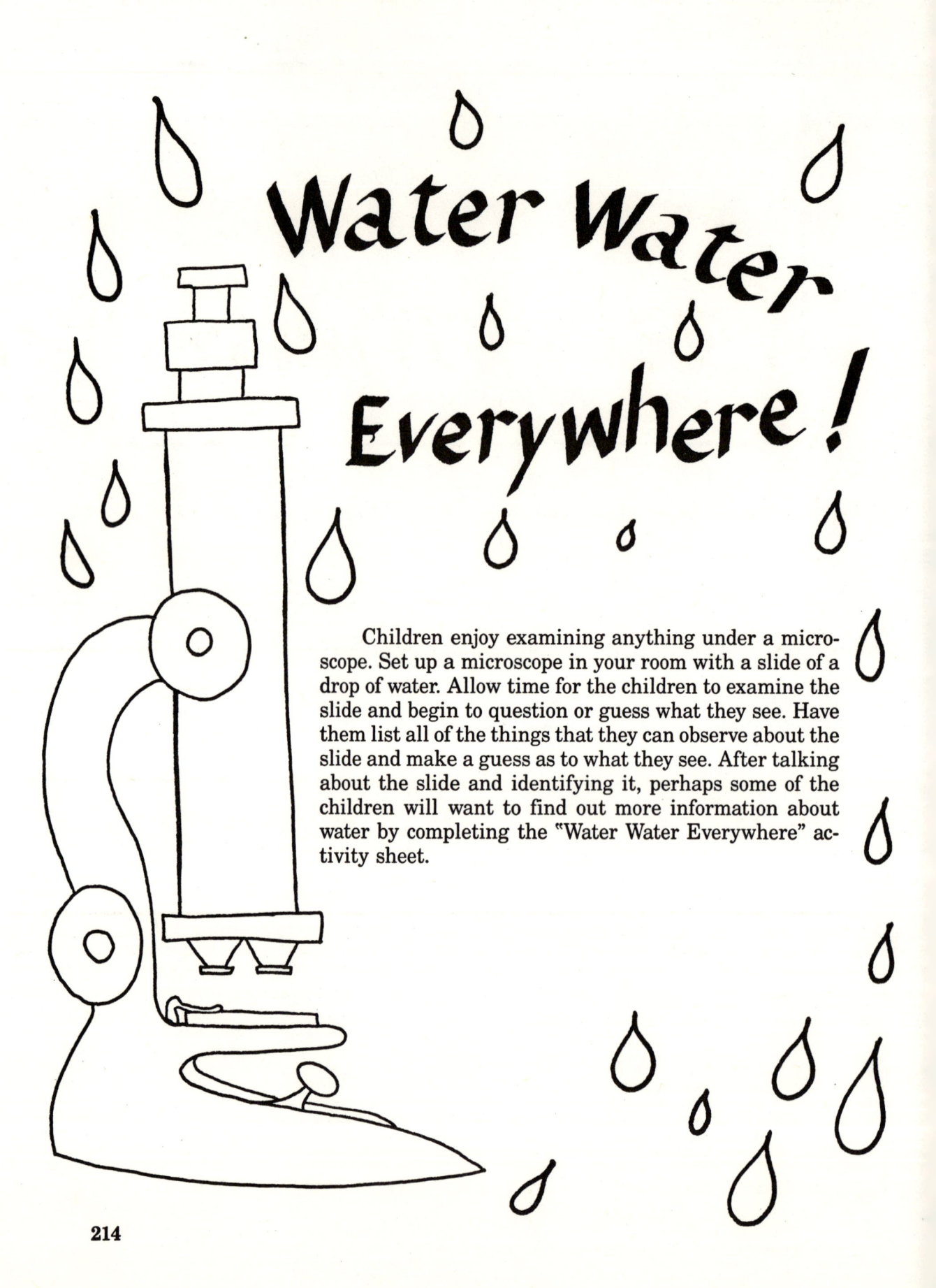

Water Water Everywhere!

Children enjoy examining anything under a microscope. Set up a microscope in your room with a slide of a drop of water. Allow time for the children to examine the slide and begin to question or guess what they see. Have them list all of the things that they can observe about the slide and make a guess as to what they see. After talking about the slide and identifying it, perhaps some of the children will want to find out more information about water by completing the "Water Water Everywhere" activity sheet.

Name _____ Date _____

Grade _____ Teacher_____

Water, Water Everywhere

A. What I already know about water. Use the back of this sheet if necessary.

_____
_____
_____
_____
_____
_____
_____
_____
_____
_____

B. Questions I want to answer about water. Put a check by three questions.
____ 1. What are the true sources of water?
____ 2. What are some of the uses of water?
____ 3. Where does water flow to and from?
____ 4. How does water work for us?
____ 6. What effect does the sun have on water?
____ 7. How does water get into the clouds?
____ 8. How do we keep our water clean?
____ 9. How much of the earth is covered by water?

215

C. How are you going to find the answers to the questions you checked about water? You may want to check:

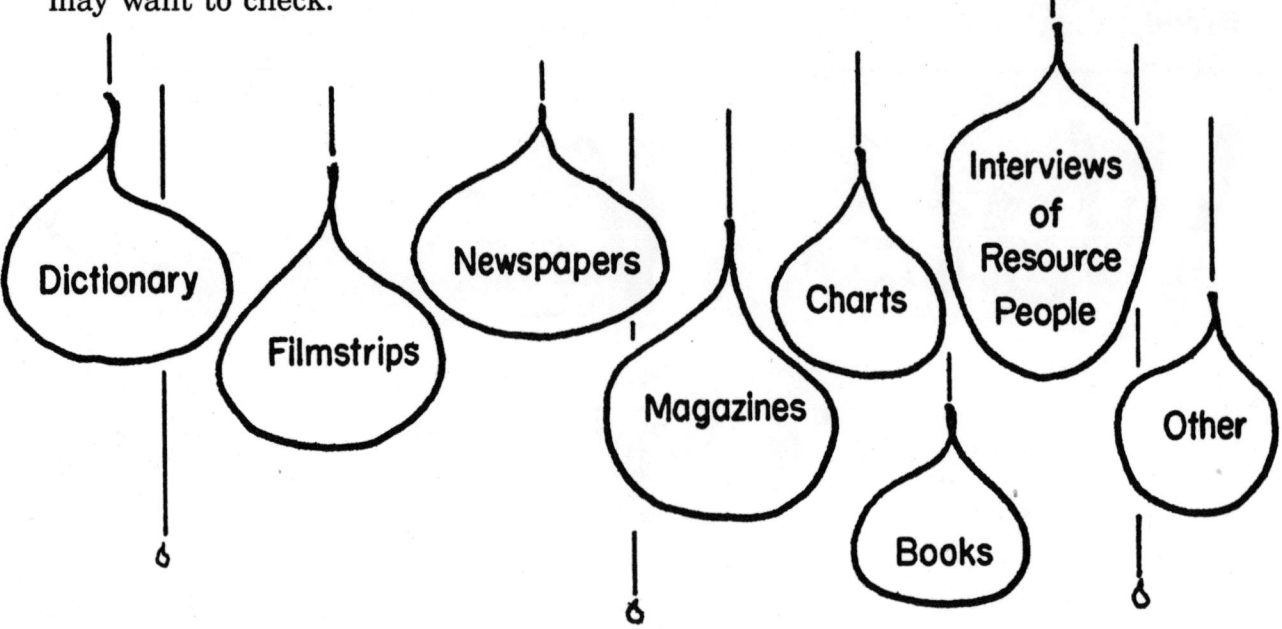

- Dictionary
- Filmstrips
- Newspapers
- Magazines
- Charts
- Books
- Interviews of Resource People
- Other

Color the water droplets as you explore and find the answers to the questions you chose.

D. Share the answers that you found with your class. You may want to try one of these ways or one of your own!

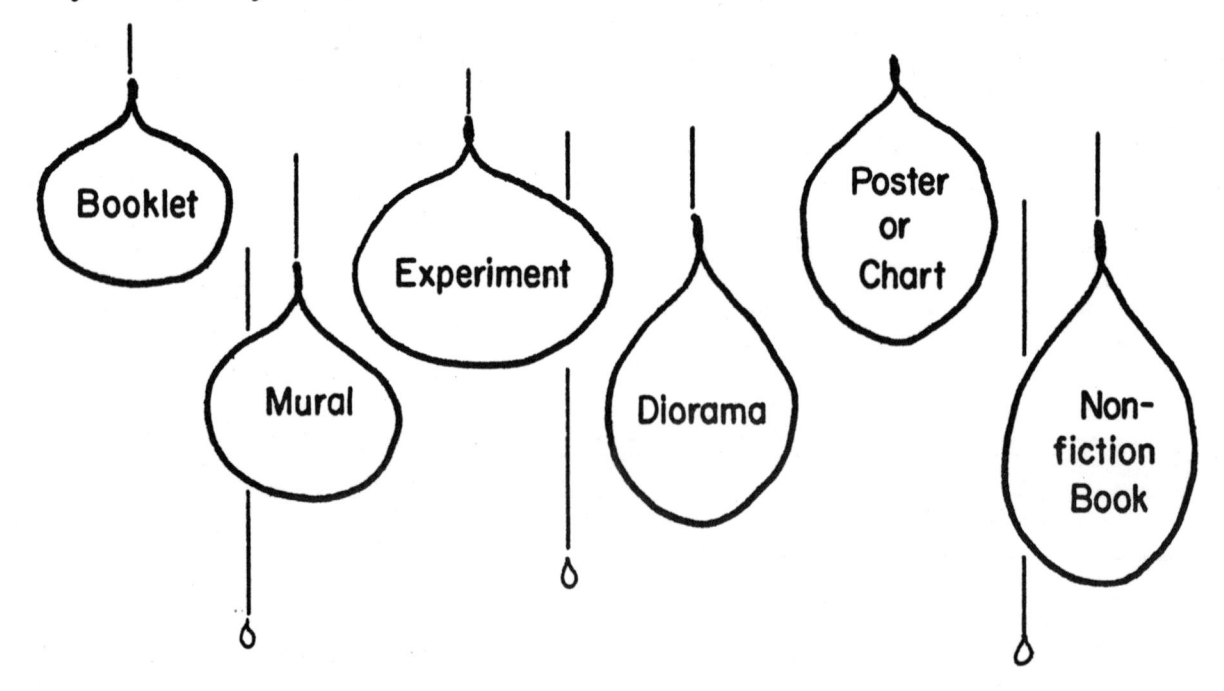

- Booklet
- Mural
- Experiment
- Diorama
- Poster or Chart
- Non-fiction Book

E. Did you enjoy finding out about water on your own?

What did you like most?
Why?
Do you want to do another study?
What subjects interest you?

HOW WELL DID YOU DO?

- EXCELLENT
- VERY GOOD
- GOOD
- FAIR

COLOR THE WATER DROPLET TO SHOW HOW WELL YOU DID.

TALL PLANS

Name

Date

Materials I will need:

Activities I will do:

1.

2.

3.

How do you measure up? Color in the giraffe to show how well you feel you did.

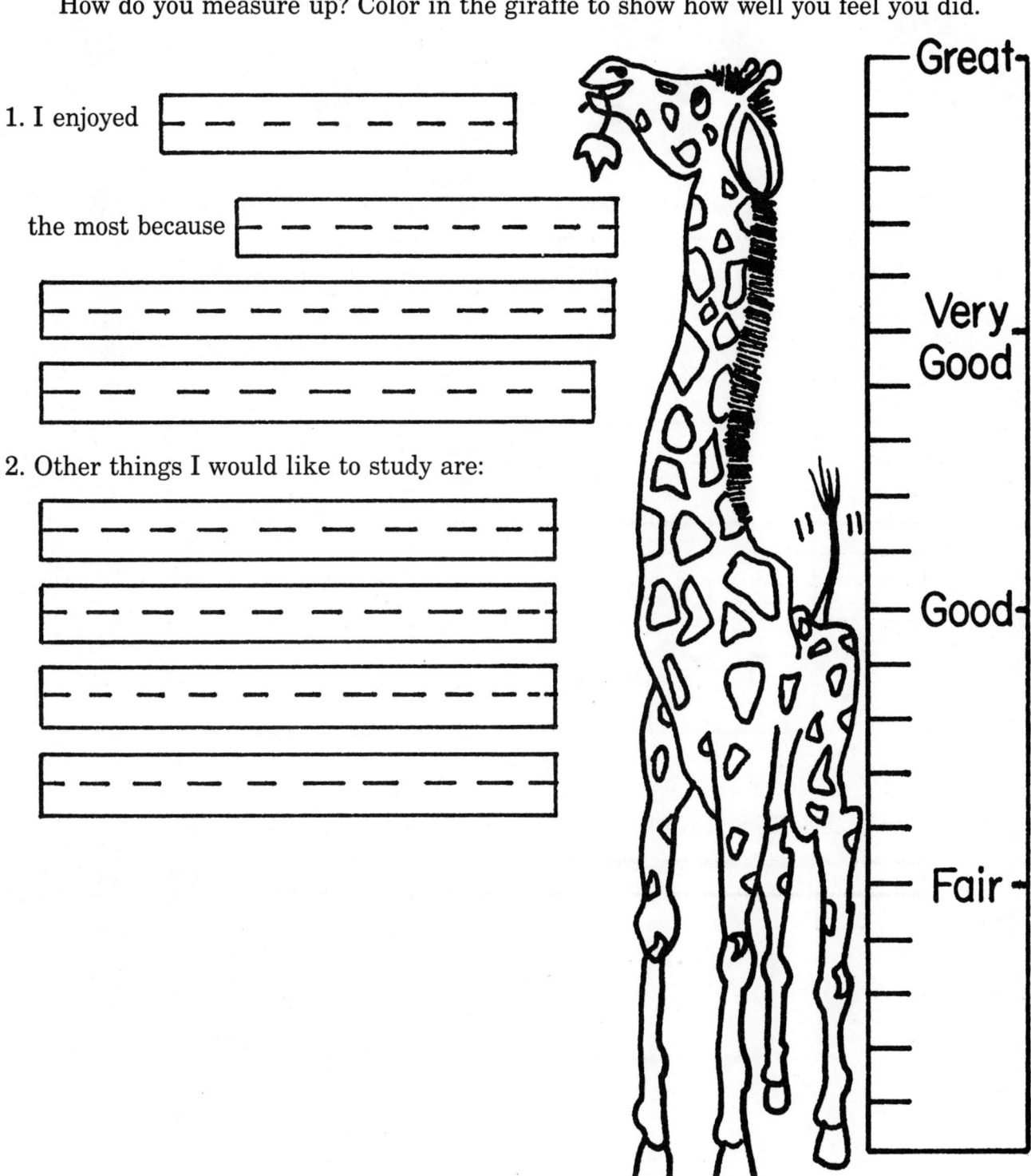

1. I enjoyed

the most because

2. Other things I would like to study are:

Great

Very Good

Good

Fair

Name _____   Date _____

Choosing A Career

Directions: Answer the questions and complete the activities below.

1. Using a large piece of chart paper, make a list of as many careers as you can think of. Leave some space between each career so that you can complete Step 2. Here is an example.

```
         Careers
   1. Doctor
   2. Lawyer
   3. Firefighter
```

2. Now, beside each career that you have listed, write any special training, tools, etc., you might need to carry out this career. For example:

```
              Careers
   1. Doctor – Medical School Training
```

© 1985 by The Center for Applied Research in Education, Inc.

3. From your list, choose three careers you are interested in finding out more about. Write them here.

1. _____

2. _____

3. _____

4. Go to the library and find out more about each of these careers. Try to decide which of the three careers you are most interested in. Write your choice here.

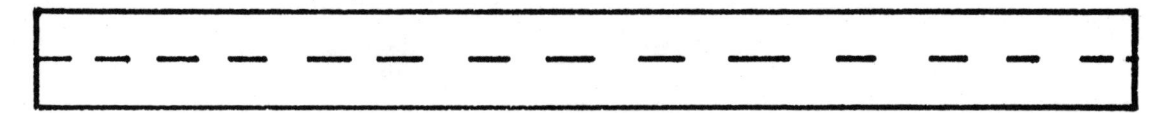

_____

5. Make a job fact sheet about your career choice. For example:

> **CHEF**
> 1. cooks in a restaurant
> 2. has to be well-organized
> 3. has to know math to be able to increase or decrease a recipe

6. Using the "My Interview of a _____" sheet, try to interview one person about the career you selected. Be sure to thank that person for the interview.

221

7. **Make a career collage.** Using magazine pictures, small objects, cloth, newspaper headlines, etc., create a collage about the career you have selected. Be sure to include as many ideas from your fact sheet as you can. (**HINT:** A collage can be three-dimensional. Talk to your teacher for ideas.) Here is an example:

8. Share your career choice, facts about your career, and collage with your class.

MY INTERVIEW OF A _____

NAME _____

I interviewed _____ on
               NAME

_____
    DATE

Questions To Ask:

1. What is the title of your job?
   _____
   _____

2. What kind of special training did you need?
   _____
   _____

3. What are some important duties of your job?
   _____
   _____
   _____
   _____

4. Do you wear a special uniform for your job? If yes, what?
_____
- - - - - - - - - - - - - - - - - -
_____

5. Do you use any special tools in your job? If yes, what?
_____
- - - - - - - - - - - - - - - - - -
_____

6. What do you like most about your job?
_____
- - - - - - - - - - - - - - - - - -
_____
- - - - - - - - - - - - - - - - - -
_____

7. What is the most frustrating part of your job?
_____
- - - - - - - - - - - - - - - - - -
_____
- - - - - - - - - - - - - - - - - -
_____

Name _____ Date _____

CAREERS OF THE FUTURE

1. Make a chart listing all of the careers you can think of. Leave a space between each career.

2. Now, look at your list carefully. Decide which of the careers you think will still be necessary in 100 years. Mark an X beside each of these careers.

3. Explain how the careers that you did not mark with an X will be replaced in the future. Here is an example:

    Waitress—replaced by a robot.

4. Invent a career of the future. Write a description of the job you would like to have. Tell what you think you would do and what kind of training you would need. Be sure to include what you think you would wear, what your hours would be, etc. You can use the "My Career of the Future" activity sheet to complete this.

My Career of the Future

My career of the future would be

- - - - - - - - - - - - - - - - -

- - - - - - - - - - - - - - - - -

- -

- -

- -

- -

- -

- -

- -